Do Not Adjust Your Set

Do Not Adjust Your Set

Kate Dunn

John Murray

© Kate Dunn 2003

First published in 2003 by John Murray (Publishers)
A division of Hodder Headline

The moral right of the author has been asserted

A CIP catalogue record for this title is available from the British Library

ISBN 0-7195-5480 2

Typeset in Baskerville by Servis Filmsetting Ltd, Manchester

Printed and bound in Great Britain by Clays Ltd, St Ives plc

John Murray (Publishers)
338 Euston Road
London
NW1 3BH

For Tom and Stella

Contents

Illustrations

The author and publishers would like to thank the following for permission to reproduce illustrations: Plates, 1, 3, 4, 5, 8, 10, 11 and 12, BBC Photograph Archive; 2 and 7, Hulton Archive; 6, BBC Written Archive; 9, Leonard Lewis.

Acknowledgements

I AM EXTREMELY grateful to the actors, actresses, directors, writers and technicians who ransacked their memories to provide me with the wonderful stories that make up this book. They were all generous with their time, their insights and in many cases their personal archives; and their good sense of humour and forebearance made researching *Do Not Adjust Your Set* a pleasure. I am particularly indebted to Sir Nigel Hawthorne, Peggy Mount, Maurice Denham and John Warner, all of whom were kind enough to grant me interviews when they were coping with serious illnesses during the last months of their lives. I hope that the anecdotes they passed on to me will serve as a celebration of the enormous contribution they made to television.

I would like to say a big thank you to the Actors' Charitable Trust and the Frances Head Memorial Fund for their benevolent support during the long period of working on this book.

I am greatly indebted to the BBC Written Archive Centre, and in particular Jeff Walden for his help in guiding me through the fantastic collection of written material about the early days of television that is held there. The archivist Jacquie Kavanagh has been most kind in allowing me to quote from BBC material, and I would also like to express my thanks to Miss Waveney S.C. Holt for allowing me to include passages from *Savoy Hill and Portland Place*, the memoir of her father Edgar C. Holt. Extracts from *Playback*, Dallas Bower's autobiography, by kind permission of Delian Bower. Robin Esser has generously allowed me to quote an article from the *New Chronicle* and I am indebted to Andrew Crisell for permitting me to include excerpts from his excellent book *An Introductory History of British Broadcasting* (London, Routledge, 1997). I have been unable to trace the copyright holders for *Television is for All* by the late Leonard Marsland Gander, published by Alba, but would be very pleased to hear from them and in the meantime hope that they will not object to my using a brief extract from his work.

Caroline Knox, Hazel Wood and Vicki Harris at John Murray have been of inestimable help during the complex process of putting this narrative together and I am most appreciative of their tact and thoughtfulness. I am also grateful to Sarah Molloy for the back-up she has given me.

Finally, I would like to thank my parents for their unswerving support; Carole Pugh, Nicola West, Sue Regan and Chris Simmonds for getting me out of the occasional tight spot; Nick Shearman, Janie Hampton, Sarah Steindl, Vicky Allen and Jonathan Dockar-Drysdale for their many contributions; and last (but really first) my husband Steve. A big hug to my son Jack, who wants to be in this book too!

Introduction

THE IDEA FOR *Do Not Adjust Your Set* first presented itself when I was researching my book about repertory theatre, *Exit Through the Fireplace*, a narrative constructed from the recollections of performers who had worked in regional theatre. During our conversations several actors commented that they had thought weekly rep was tough until they tackled live television. One or two people told me stories that all too clearly demonstrated this point, and it was from these reminiscences that the idea for this book began to germinate.

As I delved further into the subject, a number of parallels started to emerge. When plays were broadcast live on television, by definition they had to be done in one fell swoop – there was no facility to stop and do retakes as there was in film. Because the turnover of productions was high, the amount of rehearsal was often brief, and directors were obliged to use actors who could sustain a performance from start to finish and who were used to a minimal period of preparation. The obvious solution was to cast from a pool of actors with experience of repertory theatre.

Amongst the performers I spoke to, several were aware of similarities between the tradition in which they had been trained and the new medium they were entering. Trevor Bannister describes it as 'repertory theatre in an iron lung', and goes on to say, 'There was no question of live television being like film acting; it was like live theatre. There was no chance of saying, "I'm sorry, can I do that again?"' and that is the situation that exists on stage in a live theatre. Live television was like repertory in so far as the rehearsal period was very short.' Peggy Mount, late lamented star of both stage and television, echoed this observation: 'It was very like weekly rep, but even harder work, strangely enough, because you couldn't go back on things.' Michael Kilgarriff recalls that 'One's experience in rep did help because you were so used to things going wrong. It was your stock-in-trade not just to learn the lines but to cope with the problems,' a point with which Edward Jewesbury agrees: 'Theatre training helped with live TV – you just kept going. We rehearsed the whole thing before, had one day in studio to run through it with the camera, and then we did it.' According to Josephine Tewson, television producers were keen to exploit the unflappable attitude acquired by theatre actors: 'It was hair-raising, [but] not so bad for people who had done a lot of rep. Those first nights were always hair-raising. That's why a lot of people in *Crossroads* and *Coronation Street* in the early days were taken from the local reps, because they knew how to learn lines and deliver them in a crisis. People who hadn't done rep were just caught out, they were just too nervous and too frightened.'

Not only was a large proportion of the artists imported

from regional theatre, to begin with many of the plays that were presented live on television were staple repertory fare. It took some time for television writers to discover the unique properties of the new medium and to write specifically for it. The actor Richard Bebb claims that 'In the early days they largely did plays that were already written. As far as original writing for television was concerned, that would only have been about a fifth of the output.' So initially the approach was to point the cameras at a stage production and film it. Edward Jewesbury remembers, 'I was at the Birmingham Rep and we would take the play that we were doing at Birmingham to the Alexandra Palace. On the Sunday morning we would go to London by coach and we would do the play on the Sunday evening. God knows what we did for scenery – we just put the play on as we were doing it at the Rep.' A glance at the illustrations in this book confirms that, in terms of content, appearance and even the style of acting, in its early days television drama borrowed heavily from the theatre, feeding upon the older tradition until it had almost totally consumed it.

Another of the links between the repertory movement and early television is that they seem to have appealed to broadly the same audience, and thus were in competition from the outset. At the outbreak of war the whole of England was dotted with thriving repertory companies – in the early 1940s there were as many as two hundred outfits of various sizes in operation, and James Grout thinks performers were so preoccupied with their work in this medium that they had no time for the new arrival. 'Television was something that was happening in the wilds of north London, in somewhere called Alexandra Palace, and it was miles away from everywhere. Everybody was busy working in the theatre: there was much more theatre than there is now, the provincial theatre was very strong, repertory was very strong, so an awful lot of actors were not anywhere near London. You wouldn't leave your job and hike to London in the hope of getting work in this strange television lark.' However, as the twenty-first century dawns only one quarter of the repertory companies that existed before the war still survive, and many people lay the blame for the demise of regional theatre at television's door. Peggy Mount stated, 'When television first came along everybody was very worried, especially theatre managements. I remember Reggie Salberg [producer of the repertory theatre at Salisbury] saying, "This is the end of the stage, we'll never be able to cope with this." They were terribly afraid of television.' But theatre director and actor Malcolm Farquhar did not feel immediately threatened: 'When television first started I think that we thought it was magic. I don't think we had any idea that it would take over the theatre. There were only so many people in the country who owned a television set. It wasn't until the mid-fifties that we noticed it was beginning to affect the theatre box office. A lot of actors were deprived of the pleasure of playing to a full house and so they went off to do television.'

This account begins with the inception of television in 1936 and covers the first thirty years of its growth. Although the technology to record material was first employed in this country in 1958, it was expensive to use and therefore slow to catch on. There was a period during the early and mid-1960s when plays were performed 'as live' – i.e. taped, but with few or no breaks, in order to avoid the cost of editing. By 1967 the conversion to recording was more or less completed. As programmes were now recorded in short segments rather than in one go, the parallel with the theatre became less pronounced and the working practices of television, as well as its end product, came to resemble film more closely. For this reason, I have chosen to end my study at this point.

In writing *Do Not Adjust Your Set*, I have concentrated on television's coverage of drama because of its obvious links with rep, and for the same reason I have largely excluded light entertainment, which derived from a parallel form of theatre, variety. These are two complementary but distinct traditions within the theatrical profession and I wanted to observe that demarcation in this book. I have not explored television's dealings with the world of sport (in spite of its inherent drama) as it represents a different form of entertainment altogether. However, I have canvassed some *presenters'* recollections of their work in live television, as a number of them have their roots firmly in the theatre.

Although many of the performers who worked in television during its early days were graduates from the rigours of repertory theatre, they look back on what they achieved when broadcasts went out live with a mixture of awe and astonishment. The distinguished theatrical veteran Paul Rogers states, 'The BBC as it was was absolutely wonderful. You didn't get paid much, the conditions under which you worked weren't wonderful, but you got the feeling throughout the organization that it was exciting. People were trusted, and it was not being run by accountants. That's the bitter and terrible truth of today. People were not looking over their shoulders, petrified of what was going to happen. There was a certain amount of licence, of course there was. But that was kind of expected by the high-ups, they expected people to make a bosh of it from time to time. Experiment and discovery were part and parcel of the job.' Peter Bowles confirms that a pioneering atmosphere prevailed. 'Doing live television was a new form of work really. I imagine it was rather like working on a ship when it was under attack – "Action stations!" There was a feeling of everyone donning their flak jackets and lifebelts.' The actor John Warner echoed this war-like imagery; 'As they started the countdown, ten, nine, eight, seven, all the way down to nought, your heart was pounding so much it was like going over the top in the trenches.'

Like its forerunner, *Do Not Adjust Your Set* is drawn from personal recollections of the actors and actresses who were directly involved. This sets it apart from the existing canon of excellent works about the broadcasting media that are based on written sources. What oral history is able to offer in particular is insight from people with first-hand experience of the subject. An actor who was a regular performer in *Z Cars* will have access to information about television in the 1960s that a conventional historian will not. He will be able to speak with authority about the shortage of rehearsal time, the relationship with the director, the dynamics with other cast members, not to mention the pressures of working live in studio. Because his recollections are oral, they have a spontaneity and immediacy that much written archive material lacks. In this way oral histories are different in both perspective and tone from more formal studies. They can also be more democratic. Although I have interviewed many of the great and the good of the theatrical profession to plunder their memories, I have also talked to people whose names do not appear in lights, in order to ensure that their voices are heard as well. It is the ordinary people who often fail to make an impact in more conventional histories and I hope that this book will be even-handed in representing artists from all tiers of the business.

However, the subjectivity that is a virtue of oral history can also be its undoing – memories are sometimes faulty, any group of people will express different points of view about the same situation or subject, and many recollections become exaggerated with retelling. Some of the people I interviewed were aware of this: the writer Dick Sharples said, 'I'm trying to remember the true stories, rather than the ones that have been polished over the years.'

In 1791 Jane Austen wrote a brief history of England which she said was written 'By a partial, prejudiced and ignorant Historian', adding, 'N. B. There will be very few Dates in this History.' This book is offered up in the same informal spirit. My intention has been to capture the humour and wit of the contributors, as well as their intelligence, their wisdom and the breadth of their experience. The narrative is intended to be intimate, confiding and chatty. It is my hope that, although this account may occasionally be idiosyncratic, it will not only provide insight into actors' experience of working in the earliest days of television but also demonstrate how they helped to shape a medium that has so radically altered the way we experience our lives.

1

The Early Days of Television 1936–9

In 1925 the Scottish electrical engineer John Logie Baird gave the first demonstration of a television transmission, in the London department store Selfridges. But the earliest experiments into how to transmit a combination of visual and audio signals had followed two separate paths. The first of these, pioneered by the German scientist Paul Nipkow in 1884 and later pursued by Baird, involved a mechanical means of scanning images using a revolving disc with small perforations in it that projected patterns of dots for transmission. The second approach was not mechanical but instead was rooted in electronics. Karl Braun invented the cathode ray tube in 1897; the photo-electric cell was devised by Hans Geitel and Julius Elster in 1905; and eighteen years later the Russian-born American scientist Vladimir Zworykin invented the iconoscope, a form of electronic camera. The American companies RCA and EMI poured a huge amount of funding into the electronic line of research and development, but they were pipped to the post by Baird, who achieved a couple of notable firsts during the 1920s. As well as his coup in Selfridges, in 1928 he trounced the Americans by sending the first television signal across the Atlantic. To counter this, in the same year the United States saw the first ever test television programme, a cartoon of *Felix the Cat*.

The British Broadcasting Corporation had been incorporated under Royal Charter in 1927. This confirmed its monopoly as the state provider of radio programmes and established the basic principles of its working ethos. The BBC's brief was to inform, to educate and to entertain. It had obligations to broadcast proceedings in Parliament and to maintain political balance. In the event of national emergency, it was to convey government information to the people. As the national broadcaster the Corporation had an interest in the development of television, and an association with Baird was formed when the Post Office asked it to give him the facilities to work on his transmissions. 'The Baird Television Development Company had done some experiments in drama from its studio in Long Acre, notably a programme called *The Man With a Flower in His Mouth* by Pirandello, but the first really substantial association of the Corporation with television took place on 22nd August 1932, when the Baird system started operating a regular service from the bowels of Broadcasting House in Portland Place,' wrote Dallas Bower, an early television producer. However, a year later the Corporation switched its support to what by then appeared to be the superior system, the electronic one offered by Marconi EMI from America.

By the time the BBC Television Service was officially launched in 1936, a government committee under Lord Selsdon, briefed to consider the future of television broadcasting, had advised that both the mechanical and the electronic systems should be used in tandem, week in, week out, until one of them emerged as the clear favourite. This meant that when the opening broadcast was made on the afternoon of 2 November 1936 from Alexandra Palace in north London, a site chosen because its elevated position would enhance the transmission of the signal, the first pro-gramme went out between 3 and 4 p.m. from the Baird studio, and then was repeated between 4 and 4.30 p.m. from the Marconi EMI studio.

This arrangement, unsurprisingly, proved to be both limiting and awkward. Dallas Bower comments, 'Alternate weeks were to be devoted to Baird and EMI respectively. From a purely production point of view the EMI (elec-tronic) system worked and the Baird (mechanical) one did not. For three months we had to restrict ourselves to pro-grammes which we knew were just possible on Baird, but they bore little relation to what I understood by dramatic entertainment.'

The actress Dinah Sheridan was among the first stars to be lured to Alexandra Palace. She recalls, 'My TV appear-ances started in October 1936, when I was in the very first programme of *Picture Page* being interviewed by Leslie Mitchell, as a sixteen-year-old actress who had just made her first film as juvenile lead. This earned me the title of "the first ever actress on television".' (A record of the budget for one of the editions of *Picture Page* is still in exist-ence and throws light on the kind of costs that making programmes incurred. 'Two days studio shooting rental – £100 [roughly £2,000 today], ½ days' studio building – £15, three small stock sets from Alexandra Palace (including erection and striking) – £20. Hire of sound truck – £65, Labour (props, electricians etc) – £30, Lighting – £10, Artists and accompanist – £47, Stock, processing and re-recording costs – £103 10s. Contingency 10% – £39. Total – £429 10s. [£8,450] Transport not included.') Following the first blooding of an interview, Dinah Sheridan was contracted to appear in one of the earliest live dramas: 'I played the lead in the first three-act play ever produced on television, which was called *Gallows Glorious*. There were two studios, one with the Baird system and the other Marconi – both of which had to be used for the two sets that we needed. The rivalry between the two was very obvious, and as we did Act One in the Marconi studio we had to change costume and dash to the Baird studio for Act Two, being greeted by a fairly unfriendly crew. For Act Three we were back again in the Marconi studio. All this was of course live.' This system was not tenable for long and by February 1937 the Baird equipment had been quietly abandoned in favour of its American rival.

A broader description of the facilities available at the BBC's first television station is provided by Bower: 'In November 1936 the self-contained layout at Alexandra Palace consisted of Studio B, with the Baird mechanical system, and Studio A with the EMI electronic system, on the first floor of the south eastern block, with vision and sound transmitters feeding the unique aerial display on its mast emerging from the south east tower. This aerial was designed by the great radio engineer C. S. Franklin of the Marconi Company.' This splendid landmark mast was intended to transmit a signal over a radius of twenty-five miles. D. C. Birkinshaw, who was the television engineer in

charge during the pre-war period and was therefore intim-
ately acquainted with the mast, described its effectiveness
in a radio talk broadcast in 1944: 'Of course there were
freak receptions many miles away, and we had regular
viewers in Brighton on the south coast a good seventy miles
away.' One of the benefits of Alexandra Palace was that
'Everything was under one roof. The transmitters were on
the roof, and everything else underneath – the studios, the
control room, the administration – and that was a great
advantage. Everyone was in close touch – engineers and
producers got to know each other's problems. We engineers were always on hand to explain to producers that
they were asking for the moon.'

To begin with the new medium was obliged to draw on
existing terms of reference, according to Dallas Bower.

It is clear that the thought which had gone into planning Studio
A was in terms of 'theatre' rather than 'film'. At the extreme east
end was a well set up cyclorama, with a curtain set a third or so in
distance from its periphery, thus enclosing the equivalent of a
procenium-bound stage. The orchestra was located at the
extreme west end of the studio. The operational area was therefore the space between the orchestra's first desk of violins and
the lower run of the stage, that is to say, it was assumed all action
would be confined essentially within the stage space itself,
despite four electronic Emitron cameras. No 1 camera was
mounted on a Vinton cine-camera truck and the other three on
heavy stands known as Iron Men.

In July 1937 the *Radio Times*, in an article called 'News for
Televiewers', was keen to explain to its readers how these
cameras might be deployed. 'On the studio floor may be

four Emitrons, one trained on a caption board, another perhaps giving a profile of a pianist, a third showing a close-up of the hands on the keys, and the fourth, and most important of all, mounted on a movable truck to follow a troop of dancers. Two men have to operate this last Emitron – the cameraman himself, who sits aloft on the truck, and an assistant who manoeuvres it from one position to another.'

Ian Carmichael remembers the cramped conditions: 'If you were doing a musical you had maybe as many as three sets but also Eric Robinson and his entire orchestra in the studio with you, so there was hardly room to move. If you had to do a quick change or get on to another set it was a sort of obstacle race not to cross in front of the cameras. You had to dodge underneath them and round the back of them and step over cables.' Richard Bebb, who also acted at Alexandra Palace, recalls, 'There was a corridor of at least forty yards between the two studios at Alexandra Palace. For big drama productions they would use both studios and you often had to hare from one to the other. It was pretty primitive, but enormously exciting.' James Grout also describes the need to sprint down the corridor: 'They hadn't quite caught on to the fact that it was a good idea to have scenes that followed each other in the same studio, so sometimes you had to hare along this corridor as fast as your legs would carry you, changing your costume at the same time. An amazing number of scenes used to start with the actors out of breath.' Racing from studio to studio was not only problematic for the artists, as actress Barbara Lott relates: 'There was a director who used both of the studios at Alexandra Palace and had to go from one control box to the other. Somehow he got lost, went through a door and was never seen again.'

The *Radio Times* had been launched in 1923; it first carried a television supplement to cater for the needs of viewers as well as listeners in January 1937. On the front cover of this is a sepia photograph of the Alexandra Palace transmission mast. Amidst photographs of artists and short articles of general interest, the programmes are listed thus:

Television Programmes Monday 11 Jan and Tues 12 Jan : Vision 45 Mc/S, Sound 41.5 Mc/S. This week's transmission will be with the Baird system. Monday 3.00, British Movietone News; 3.10 Scenes from *The Soul of Nicholas Snyders*, a play by J. K. Jerome from the Arts Theatre, London; 3.25 Film, *Underground Farmers*; 3.35, Leonard Henry (comedian); 3.40, Elizabeth Schooling in *Bluebird* (Pas de deux from Tchaikovsky's *The Sleeping Beauty*;) 4.00 Close. 9.00 Repeat of Elizabeth Schooling; 9.20 Sea Stories by Commander A. B. Campbell; 9.30 Sophisticated Cabaret with Gwen Farrar; 9.50 Gaumont British News; 10.00 Close.

The schedule shows that there were only two hours of rather repetitive broadcasting a day and that the programmes rarely lasted for more than twenty minutes. (It is significant to note that the listings contained the rider, 'All programme timings shown on these pages are approximate.')

Compared to current scheduling, there is a significant lack of sport, but by March 1937 the BBC was ready to fill the gap. The *Radio Times* announced, 'March the 23rd is the Boat Race feature – John Snagge and Tom Brocklebank discussing the race, illustrated with models and films of "high spots" of boat races of the past.' Although wildly unsophisticated compared to modern coverage, the programme must have been considered a success, for the following month the *Radio Times* declared, 'On April 30 Howard Marshall will be seen as editor of a television sports review, which it is hoped will be presented regularly. Films of sporting events will be shown, together with personalities of the day.' (It was not until the mid-fifties that a number of the major sporting bodies were sufficiently confident of the technical expertise of television to allow their sports to be broadcast. They were also fearful of losing their supporters to the comfort and economy of watching matches at home. However, the tide of television proved unstoppable and in 1958 the BBC launched its flagship programme *Grandstand*, with extensive coverage of football and other sporting events.)

One of Dallas Bower's earliest jobs was to produce and direct a demonstration film that would suggest the breadth of fare available on television. This was transmitted at 11 a.m. on 26 July 1937 and included Margot Fonteyn dancing; an interview with John Piper, the painter and art critic; racing tips from the Corporation's resident expert Prince Monolulu; the Minister for Transport Leslie Hore-Belisha (inventor of the Belisha beacon) giving a talk on road safety; and appearances by Adèle Dixon and Frances Day, musical-comedy stars. The excerpts chosen for inclusion suggest that the BBC was concerned to appeal to a wide range of interests. The *Daily Telegraph* reviewed what was on offer during one of the early trials using the Baird system in November 1936, praising the way film stars Bebe Daniels and Ben Lyon adapted themselves to the demands of television. There was also a talk about the making of a model of the *Golden Hind*, the flagship of Sir Francis Drake's fleet, and a discussion on the finer points of dog-breeding, illustrated with photos lent by the Metropolitan and Essex Canine Society. The television set used by the *Telegraph* reviewer was a Cossor – the model 137T cost 106 guineas. (To put this in context, the annual salary of Jasmine Bligh, who worked as a TV announcer in 1936, was about £400.)

The staff who worked at Alexandra Palace during these early television trials were nothing if not ambitious. Following on from the success of his demonstration film, Bower seized the opportunity to screen the first classic drama production on television.

> The first Shakespeare play on television was David Garrick's version of *The Shrew*. The Garrick version was brought to my attention by Stuart Latham, who in due course was to become famous in television history as the initiator and first pro-ducer/director of *Coronation Street*. Margaretta Scott played Katherine, Austin Trevor Petruchio. We managed to secure a whole fourteen days' rehearsal. The Beaumont Mews rehearsal rooms behind the *Radio Times* and *Listener* publication building in Marylebone High Street proved to be an essential necessity in the interests of television drama. Lack of rehearsal time with the full technical crew proved to be the director's nightmare.

The choice of an established work as a subject for broad-cast seems to have been fairly typical, but an adaptation – a hybrid involving both a classic text and some original writing – was not far behind. Judy Campbell's 1938 version of *Emma* by Jane Austen shows the ambitious nature of the projects and the bravura approach to the work: 'A friend of mine called Michael Barry became the first Director of Television Drama. He asked me if I had any ideas for something I could write or adapt for television. I said, "Yes, Jane Austen's *Emma*." I'd been longing to play Emma, so I wrote it. There appeared to be no limit. We were going to have both the sound stages at Alexandra Palace. You really were running between the two, taking off your bonnet and other bits and pieces, then playing the next scene and finding that you only had one shoe on! We had a shot of Mr Knightley riding past the window, we had a quadrille in the ballroom scene, all done live. Dorothy Primrose played Harriet. There was a scene in which she played the spinet: we borrowed it and it was very heavily insured. I remember men in cloth boots coming to move it so that we could get on with the next scene. Of course they took the spinet stool away while she was standing up and she had to bend her knees to look as though she were sitting down for the next shot.'

Since its earliest days the BBC appears to have been reliant upon repeats of programmes to help fill the schedules – Judy Campbell recalls that this was common practice. 'You did a performance on Sunday and then the repeat on Thursday.' The good sense of this becomes apparent in her next comment: 'When we did the first performance of *Emma* there was a power cut right across London. We were blacked out and there was nothing that we could do about it at all.'

As the pioneers in television became more confident, the scope of what was attempted widened rapidly. Looking back during a wartime radio broadcast, the television announcer Leslie Mitchell recalled, 'We did plays, cabaret, opera, variety, fashion shows, illustrated talks and demonstrations; we put out newsreels, we visited Wimbledon tennis tournaments, the Oxford and Cambridge Boat Race, the Derby – all the major sporting events. Our cameras were present for Prime Minister Chamberlain's return from Munich, at the Coronation procession. We went to theatre first nights, to movie studios to see the stars. We went to ack-ack batteries. I could go on for ever. We were only limited by distance and that was slowly being overcome.'

Not only were the early trail-blazers coming to grips with the challenges of broadcasting from within Alexandra Palace, they were also working with some success outside the studios. The first attempt at this took place on Saturday 5 September 1936, between 12.05 and 12.13 p.m., a broadcast showing the comedian Leonard Henry leaving Alexandra Palace via the main entrance. At first all such attempts were limited by the length of cable connecting the Emitron camera to the control room, as the following memo concerning an attempt to show racing on television demonstrates: 'I have today measured the distance between the Marconi E. M. I. studio and the racecourse. I estimate that twelve thousand feet of cable will be required. This should be sufficient to reach from the studio, down the ladder, and also from the ground to wooden tower about fifteen foot high erected by the railings on the racecourse itself.' Within six months of Leonard Henry's debut, the Corporation was planning a broadcast from a sidings at the local railway station serving the Palace, and another memo of the time illustrates the rather Heath Robinson arrangements for this: 'I have instructed Mr Edwards to have a pane of glass removed from a window in the north west wall of the [Alexandra] Palace for passage of camera, microphone and lighting cables and to replace same as soon as possible after OB [outside broadcast].'

Edward Jewesbury recollects an early attempt at outside broadcasting: 'I was doing *The Ghost Train* at the Intimate Theatre in Palmers Green and Arnold Ridley, who wrote it, was appearing in it too. The cameras came down. It must have been just about their first outside broadcast; we were about half a mile from Alexandra Palace, so they could just about do it. I can't remember if we did a special performance, or if the audience was there. They used two cameras. They didn't redirect it, they just took it *en bloc*. Nobody had learned television technique then.'

However, people were learning technique pretty quickly and in May 1937 the BBC faced its greatest challenge: a whole hour had been allotted to screen the procession to Westminster Abbey for the coronation of King George VI. It was to be the longest single television programme ever. They were unable to trail cable all the way from north London, but D. C. Birkinshaw explained how the techno- logical difficulties were overcome: 'We had two ways for getting pictures back to Alexandra Palace. In the first way we had a van with a radio transmitter in it, which would send the pictures by radio on a very short wave to Alexandra Palace – or to a boosting station *en route*. There they would be fed to the main transmitters. In the second way we used underground lines. All round London the Post Office had laid a special telephone cable, and it very often happened that we could connect up to this cable from our mobile van by ordinary telephone lines.'

Technological advances were occurring rapidly and the BBC needed to appoint people of vision who would be capable of exploring all the possibilities as they presented themselves. Speaking in a wartime broadcast the well-known radio personality Donald McCullough identified Gerald Cock, who was appointed Director of Television in 1935, as a key recruit. 'At the head of every big combined operation you'll find one man who couples vision with common sense, courage with sympathy, ferocity with humour. Gerald Cock was that man. He saw a vision of the new world in which every British home could join in a most exciting adventure.' Another crucial figure was Cecil Madden, whose chief role was television Programme Organizer, although he also produced *Here's Looking at You*, the very first television programme at Alexandra Palace, in 1936, and devised the magazine programme *Picture Page*. The senior producer was George More O'Ferrall, who began his career as assistant director to Carol Reed at the Ealing Studios and later had the distinction of gaining the first television 'Oscar', awarded by the Television Society in April 1947 for his production of *Hamlet*. Royston Morley was the other senior producer and subsequently they were joined by the gifted director Michael Barry. D. H. Munro was the Production Manager and D. R. Campbell the Lighting Designer. The only woman to hold a post of power and influence was Mary Adams, Head of Television Talks and Talks Features.

This inspirational team set the tone for the rest of the employees, and Richard Bebb was among many actors who commented on the harmony that prevailed. 'Alexandra Palace had a wonderful atmosphere. There was something about live television that could never be reproduced once they started recording. There was an extraordinary sense of camaraderie between possibly one hundred people. For a large-cast production of possibly twenty-five actors there would be about seventy-five people from other professions involved. The prop men and the dressers were totally involved – you would never see a technician of any kind reading a newspaper. The atmosphere, the bonding together, the concentration of eighty people getting it as near damn right as they could was extraordinary. You might have ten tiny sets in the studio at Alexandra Palace, all crammed in, with the actors, the dressers, the prop people, the cameramen, the lighting men, the sound men and various other professions, but they would all be transfixed and concentrated, it was this group concentration.'

Peter Byrne puts the positive atmosphere down to the fact that 'We were learning together, all of us, the stage hands, the crews.' 'We were all in it together,' recalls Judy Campbell, 'we were all in this peculiar situation that was quite new to everybody and it made all the difference in the world. You were all the time discovering, trying to get a bit better, everybody was. When it was all at Ally Pally you met the same people and you got to know them. You worked with directors who had so far only worked in the theatre and it was new for them too. It's not so daunting and it's much more fun. I know a lot of people look back on the time of live television and say, "Thank God that didn't last!" – although in point of fact it must have lasted for simply yonks. But I found it fun, I really enjoyed it.' The actress Faith Brook is equally positive: 'We all worked together – actors, directors, camera and crew – with great enthusiasm and dedication. It was new and exciting, a bit of "You're where no man has been before" syndrome, and I wouldn't have missed it for the world.'

Yet because television was so novel and the people involved in it were sailing in uncharted waters, many actors were uncertain what to make of it and the profession seems to have regarded it with a certain ambivalence. According to Dallas Bower, members of the film industry showed out-right hostility to the newcomer: 'The film industry – producers, distributors and exhibitors – was in total opposition to television for fear of competition and it would not co-operate in any way whatsoever.' Ian Carmichael endorses this view: 'At that time television was very much sneered at by the film industry. If you were a named artist under contract to a film company, that company was always very reluctant to release you for a television programme. They thought that you would not come out very well, that it was a pioneering industry with no finesse about it. In a film studio you were lit awfully carefully, there was plenty of time. The lighting and the camerawork in television studios were not up to the same standard.' This sneering attitude was not confined to the film world: actors Mary Kenton and Roger Ostime both believe that the upper echelons of the theatre were dubious about the fledgeling medium as well. Kenton remarks, 'The grand people in the theatre were rather scathing about television in the early days. The big stars wouldn't do television, they only did theatre,' an opinion with which Ostime concurs: 'When I first started it was Ally Pally and the nine-inch screen. It was an exceptional thing that hardly anybody did. Your better class of actor didn't want to be seen in anything he thought was at all lowering.'

Dallas Bower, who on one occasion did an outside broadcast from the film studios at Dedham in Suffolk, cites an individual example of this lack of respect.

> We visited the set of a film in work called *The Divorce of Lady X* starring Laurence Olivier, Ralph Richardson and Merle Oberon. We rehearsed what I thought to be a suitable excerpt for television and which to my surprise and horror Olivier decided to 'send up' during the actual transmission. Olivier's closest friend Richardson was furious. He considered such behaviour totally unprofessional and insisted upon Olivier writing a letter of apology. Olivier's behaviour, Richardson insisted, might have got me the sack . . . a letter of apology duly arrived and the matter was never referred to again.

According to Glyn Houston, this negativity wasn't necessarily rooted in snobbery, but was more pragmatic in origin. He puts it down to the matter of hard cash. 'When television started, they decided the money would be based on radio fees. People wouldn't touch live television in those days because it was too risky and very badly paid, so people like myself were given these lovely parts. I'd go from playing a punch-drunk boxer to playing the Prince of Wales!'

The actor Peter Bowles suggests that the BBC traded upon performers' desire for exposure to the widest possible audience. 'The main feeling about television, and the BBC were great exploiters of this, disgracefully so, was that it was a good shop window. You were being seen by a lot of people and therefore you should be grateful that you were getting this exposure – you might get a job in the theatre! You weren't paid very much and your great excitement was that your mum was going to see you.'

Many performers were unsure what attitude to take towards television, amongst them James Grout: 'We thought of it as a bit of a joke, something that was not going to last. I got paid about £20 and that was quite welcome. It was still very experimental, especially the drama, and nobody quite knew how to do it.' The actor Stephen Hancock echoes this thought: 'Dare I say it, television was a bit of a joke. In those days it was something that you did when you didn't have anything better to do, the theatre was the thing. This new television business was a time filler.' Miriam Karlin recalls the reaction of her contemporaries when she admitted she was going to work at Alexandra Palace. 'I'll always remember sitting in the Arts Theatre Club with some friends, making one cup of coffee last for four or five hours, and I remember chums saying to me, "What are you doing at the moment?" "I'm doing a television," said I with great glee, and the pitying look I got from the person I said it to was as if I was doing some really grotty fringe in the sticks. And I said, "I think it's the coming thing." I remember so distinctly saying, "I'm sure it is going to be the future." It was rather like when one used to think, *God, these people who do commercials!* One used to think they were the absolute pits, how could anyone stoop that low? Now, I would kill for a commercial!'

Television was very slow to catch on, partly because the

signal could only be received in an area fairly close to Alexandra Palace. This was still the case in the period immediately after the war: 'In 1948 television was just opening up,' remembers Ian Carmichael. 'I did quite a lot at that time, but my parents, who lived in Hull, were never able to see any of it because the signal didn't reach that far. You could only receive television in the London and Home Counties area. I think they could just get it at Brighton. Not everybody had telly. While I was doing all this television I couldn't afford a telly of my own. My wife would go round to somebody else's house to watch it.' In 1949 the signal was extended to the West Midlands, but it was not able to reach Scotland, Wales or the West Country until 1952, and inevitably this limited the size of the audience. Another deterrent was the cost of sets. Given that £100 at that time would comfortably purchase a small car, the 115 guineas that HMV charged for a television (plus £27 purchase tax) was very steep. According to the *Strand* magazine, in 1949 HMV produced a combined TV-radio-gramophone for £336 including purchase tax, but average prices ranged from £60 to £100, with an additional £10 for aerial installation. There were however more economical sets available – Pye made one for £48. 17s. 3d. including tax, and GEC had a model priced at 42 guineas, with purchase tax £10. 0s. 8d. extra. Roger Ostime describes these luxury items: 'We lived in Maidstone and the people in the flat above us had a television set. It was the size of a refrigerator with a little screen at the top. It was really a talking point – "You must come up some time and see the news." It was a great rarity then.' James Grout remarks that 'You were lucky to have one television set in the road.

Nobody had it. People used to invite you in, they used to have enormous front-room parties just to watch this box. Nobody was concerned about performances or if the play was good, they were just gobsmacked at seeing it. They were huge walnut cabinets with a screen about six inches wide in the middle of them. I think the polished walnut cabinets were a hangover from the days of radiograms.' In *Television For All*, a pamphlet published shortly after the war, Leonard Marsland Gander tackles the challenge to aesthetics that the television set provided. 'The television set also raises a new problem in household decoration. Some receivers conceal the actual screen behind shutters or under a lid. The majority provide a flat surface which plainly, like a mantelpiece, demands some ornament and is a challenge to housewives' ingenuity. In my home a bowl of flowers usually stands on the television set and, with lighting behind, looks most attractive.'

With so few people able to watch, Edward Jewesbury says, 'Before the war it was just a joke because we knew that only about twelve people in the whole country had a set. You wondered if anybody was watching at all – probably not.' Maurice Denham was marginally more upbeat: 'I remember doing *Hay Fever* on Christmas Day of 1938. I think there were only thirty-six sets in the whole of London watching it.' By comparison, Dinah Sheridan is positively generous in her assessment: 'After the second showing of *Gallows Glorious* I remember standing high on the steps of Alexandra Palace looking at the vast panorama of London, with its twinkling lights, and wondering how many of those houses had a TV set and had seen what we had just done. Probably less than a hundred.' Michael

Barry, who as a television director was probably better placed to know, estimated in his book *From the Palace to the Grove* that in April 1938 the average audience consisted of twelve hundred viewers.

However, the presenter Leslie Mitchell believed that the pre-war audience was far larger. 'In and around London we could count on a hundred thousand regular home viewers (as we used to call them), that is counting three or four viewers to a set. And that doesn't take into account many thousands who watched our regular programmes in the big stores, at the radio dealers, and the many pubs that had got television sets in their saloon bars.' The tendency to watch television in public places is confirmed in the *Radio Times* article 'What the Viewers Are Saying' on 26 March 1937: 'In the big department stores, where the television room or theatre is still a novelty, there are still large crowds every day, though the numbers have dropped since the beginning of the year, when special arrangements had to be made to control the crowds.' The presenter Adrian Cairns saw his first broadcast at a hotel: 'In the 1930s Alexandra Palace only had a transmission area of about twenty-five miles. In 1936 or '37 my mother took my sister and me to see this new thing called television by having a cup of tea in the Brent Cross Hotel.'

Jean Bartlett, a correspondent to the *Radio Times* in June 1937, was one of the lucky few who possessed their own sets, although this was not always a source of pride to her.

Some of our friends, having seen it once, sometimes enquire sympathetically, as if it were an invalid member of our family, how it is getting on, and then fade away to the cinema. But the loss is theirs. The most important element of television is obviously movement. The artists may be shatteringly beautiful, the lighting perfect, the scenery just right, but without constant movement it completely fails . . . Talks are by unanimous vote the weakest point . . . the subject of the talk may be profoundly interesting, but close-up studies of the speaker's face add nothing to it, one talk of pottery was so dead that we blushed in the darkness, having invited some critical people to their first experience of television.

Another account which also smacks of dissatisfaction is to be found in 'What the Viewers Are Saying'.

The particular transmission I saw was a disappointing demonstration. The newsreels and the excerpts from films came over alright, even though they looked like postage stamp editions of the real thing in the cinema. It was the direct television that was so disappointing. Time and time again there would be a close-up of the announcer on screen, then the picture would fade or the sound would be strangled. There would follow an apology for the breakdown and for long spells there would be a blank screen and gramophone music to pass the time. In one of the fleeting moments of animation on the screen I remember the announcer saying, with what seemed to be a note of triumph in his voice, 'This is direct television from Alexandra Palace.' He brought Jack Hilton, who'd just returned from his American tour, to the screen. This was the first really significant hint of the surprises in store for television viewers, but no sooner had he begun to speak than the picture and the sound faded. It was all so tantalising.

In his wartime broadcast, Leslie Mitchell was able to throw some insight into how unnerving such situations could be for the poor television announcer concerned. 'If anything goes wrong in the studio, the announcer is put on the screen to keep things going. We – the announcers – also had to act as stooges for a variety of wild beasts that were brought to the studio from London Zoo and elsewhere; take part in various demonstrations by the London Fire Brigade; climb up hundred-foot ladders; fall into bathing pools; take off in helicopters, and what-have-you. And of course we were required never to look surprised, dismayed or agonised. It was quite a life. One of the most disconcerting commentaries I ever gave was when the London Fire Brigade brought along their newest turntable ladder for a demonstration. I volunteered to stand on top of the ladder while they extended it to its full height, and give a running commentary on my reactions to the experience. It started rather badly because almost as soon as they began to extend the ladder my trousers caught in the mechanism and began to rip slowly but inexorably from the turn-up up. The powerful engine drowned my cries of protest and I spent an agonizing few minutes literally having the pants taken off me.'

The late Nigel Hawthorne also recalled some of the frustration of watching television on the earliest sets. 'Reception was always so bad in those days. You used to have one of those aerials on top of the television, or a coat hanger stuck in it, and you had to keep moving it around. It was terribly Heath Robinson.' Apparent hitches in transmission were sometimes deliberate, according to the director Richard Digby Day: 'My first memory of watching live television was seeing Phyllis Nielsen Terry play Lady Catherine de Burgh in *Pride and Prejudice* and they had to keep switching the sound off because she couldn't remember the words.'

An article in the *News Chronicle* of 24 November 1936

conjures up the sense of occasion that imbued these early viewing experiences.

> We sat, in semi-darkness, about seven feet from the screen, and I have since found that this is the ideal distance for seeing clearly and comfortably. Once adjusted and tuned in, there was no more knob-twiddling to be done. We just sat back and enjoyed the programme. Just imagine what it means to have television in your own home. Here I am, fifteen miles from Alexandra Palace, watching on a screen ten by eight inches, a brilliant black and white picture of all that is going on in the studio. The images are so clear that I can count a man's teeth when he laughs. We watch films, including *Movietone News*; see ping pong matches; boxing bouts; excerpts from plays; jugglers, singers and so on. We become so interested in the various shows that we forget it is television, forget the wonder of it. I find the set very easy to operate. Switch on to 'Television'. The set warms up and the screen glows a little. Then tune in (a single knob tunes sound and vision). Almost immediately a flickering image comes on the screen, sways about and finally settles down into a good steady picture. Simultaneously the loud speaker blares forth. Finally there is a knob I can adjust to make the picture brighter or duller and another labelled 'Contrast' which controls the degree of black and white. There is also the usual volume control for sound. What could be simpler?

In spite of the glitches, the writer of the *Radio Times* article 'What the Viewers Are Saying' was able to report that 'Wherever I went I found that viewers were agreeably surprised by the technical excellence of television, both of transmission and of reception. It was on questions of policy and programmes that one heard criticism. It was a general complaint that there are only two one-hour trans-missions daily.'

Even this measly two hours per day was soon to be withdrawn. The BBC was very clear that it would not continue to broadcast its television service in the event of war, since the government was concerned that the distinctive masts at Alexandra Palace would provide enemy bombers with a landmark by which to pilot themselves to central London. As the prospect of conflict with Germany drew ever closer, Dallas Bower recalls that 'it was hinted to staff that we should start thinking in terms of the armed services'.

2

Wartime 1939–45

ON 3 SEPTEMBER 1939 Chamberlain decided to break the news of the declaration of war to the nation by means of the radio, having already closed down the television service. The choice of the wireless over newspapers was an indication of how vital the medium was to be in the government's management of the conflict. During the six years that followed, radio not only continued to be a key means of disseminating public-service information but also played a crucial role in maintaining the morale of the people, particularly in the early days of hostilities when cinemas, theatres and other entertainment outlets were all closed. It is perhaps for this reason that the actress Barbara Lott makes the observation that 'Life was ruled by the radio during the war.'

Although it could be argued that radio achieved its finest hour between 1939 and 1945, both its roots and its achievements extend back to the end of the nineteenth century. In 1895 the Italian physicist Guglielmo Marconi discovered a means of converting sounds into electric signals that could be transmitted to a receiver, which would change them back into sounds. In spite of his landmark achievement with early transmissions, Marconi felt that he was undervalued in his own country and moved to Britain, where he established the Wireless Telegraphy and Signal Company. In 1901 he managed to send a signal across the Atlantic, and in recognition of his pioneering work he was awarded the Nobel Prize for Physics in 1904. Only ten years later the first transatlantic transmission of speech occurred. As this was in 1914, it is perhaps not surprising that the advance of radio as a mass medium was hampered by the perception of a conflict of interests between the use of the airwaves for entertainment and for military purposes. However, with the conclusion of the First World War, the manufacturers of radio receivers were able to put a convincing argument to the British government that unless a proper service was established for people to listen to, the market would not expand. By February 1922 the Marconi company was making weekly transmissions from a radio station at Writtle in Essex, and in November of that year the government formalized arrangements and instructed the Post Office to issue a licence to a conglomerate of radio manufacturers that would henceforth be known as the British Broadcasting Company. The nascent BBC made its first ever broadcast on 14 November 1922, when Arthur Burrows, who was the Marconi company's Head of Publicity, read a news bulletin which he concluded with unscripted joviality: 'You know, this broadcasting is going to be jolly good fun.'

The early radios were known as crystal sets and by today's standards were complicated affairs for the user. One cable linked the aerial to the receiver, another connected it to the earth and a third ran to a set of headphones through which the broadcast could be heard. The apparatus was limited because only one person could listen at a time and for this reason research was quickly focused on how to reach a wider audience. The solution came with the invention of the valve radio, which replaced the crystal with vacuum tubes or valves, electric components that amplified the weak signal picked up by the receivers, so that the listener's headphones could be dispensed with. This surge of activity in the field of sound broadcast ran in parallel to the work carried out by Nipkow, Braun, Geitel, Elster, Zworykin and Baird, who were all experimenting in the related area of picture transmission. The two strands of research were broadly synchronous and complementary, and once the wireless service was established Marconi linked up with the American company EMI to start producing television equipment.

Progress in the 1920s and early thirties was not limited to the field of technology, for during this period programme makers were laying the foundation of a service that is still recognizable in the twenty-first century. Funded by the introduction of a ten-shilling licence fee, they were quickly able to provide their audience with a varied diet. In 1922 the first radio play was transmitted, the first religious address was made and *Children's Hour* was heard for the first time. The following year saw the inclusion of the first ever radio talk, by G. K. Chesterton on Burns Night, and the first live debate (of a motion that 'Communism would be a danger to the good of the people'). The following year also saw the advent of the *Afternoon Talk For Women*, whose opening episode featured an interview with Princess Alice and which eventually evolved into the *Woman's Hour* that is still known and loved today. Add to this the presentation of dance-music programmes and a regular weather forecast and it is understandable that the company saw the need to publish a weekly guide to what was on offer in the shape of the *Radio Times*, particularly as the newspapers, as part of a general policy of non-cooperation, were refusing to publish such information themselves. At the same time BBC engineers worked out a means to broadcast from outside the studio, with a ground-breaking transmission of *The Magic Flute* from Covent Garden. The facility for outside broadcasts meant that in 1924 they were able to devise programmes of such originality as the live transmission of a nightingale singing in a Surrey wood accompanied by the cellist Beatrice Harrison. That year also saw the start of signature sounds like the Greenwich pips and the chimes of Big Ben.

All these programmes reached the nation from stations around the country, each one having its own wavelength and individual call sign – London's was 2LO, Aberdeen's was 2BD, Birmingham's was 5IT, and so on. This early dependence on the regions to disseminate the signal was to have a profound effect on the subsequent structure of the BBC. At the outbreak of war, for example, a number of the Corporation's administrative departments were moved out of harm's way in London to the provinces. Centres were established in Oxford, Evesham, Bristol, Bangor, Manchester and Glasgow. When in 1967 the BBC opened the first formally constituted local radio station, based in Leicester, this set in motion a trend that has seen the regional structure being broken down into a more localized service. While regional radio continues to this day to be an important producer of drama within the BBC, regional television has made its presence felt more prominently in terms of current affairs – every part of the country still has its own local television news.

When the British Broadcasting Company was launched it had no permanent home and was temporarily based at the headquarters of the General Electrical Company in Magnet House on Kingsway in London. The transmitter was at Marconi House until 1925, when a larger model was constructed on the roof of Selfridges department store. At this stage the staff consisted of seven people under the general management of one John Reith. Such was the shortage of personnel that the Station Director, Stanton Jefferies, and his assistant Rex Palmer presented *Children's Hour* every day at 5 p.m. as Uncle Jeff and Uncle Rex. The few artistes who could be lured into appearing on 2LO were generally not paid for their services. Premises were soon found at Savoy Hill and the newly established Corporation stayed there until moving into purpose-built accommodation at Broadcasting House in Portland Place in 1932.

The move to Portland Place was not without controversy. Eric Gill had sculpted a statue of Prospero and Ariel for the façade, but the size of Ariel's penis caused such public outrage that a Member of Parliament who lived in the vicinity demanded in the House of Commons that the statue should be removed because it was 'objectionable to public morals and decency'.

Writer and broadcaster Norman Painting, who holds the world record for the portrayal of a character in a series for his evocation of Philip Archer in BBC Radio's flagship programme *The Archers*, which has lasted for more than fifty years, has early memories of visiting Broadcasting House. 'There was a certain cachet about the BBC, they were three magic letters in my childhood. Whenever you arrived at wherever it was, it was always called Broadcasting House. A sort of debutante would meet you, ask you your name and escort you to the studio. They were frightfully county. That was the way it was. It's very different now. It was always trying to be slightly grand in a with-it sort of way.'

Eric Maschwitz, who was the first Head of Variety, described the personnel as 'a mixed bohemian flock, with Reith as a strange but kindly shepherd'. Reith himself had the reputation for being a rather dour Scotsman, possessed of exacting moral principles. He seems to have set great store by a strict dress code, famously requesting that announcers should wear evening dress, even though they could not be seen by the public, in order to lend a sense of occasion to broadcasts. In the same vein he also sent a memo to engineers asking them not to show their braces if there were visitors around. Edgar Holt was the first news journalist employed by the Corporation, specifically for the changeover from Reuters to BBC-written bulletins, and his manuscript memoir conveys a sense of Reith's stature within the organisation.

> I remember one charming piece of routine which then prevailed: this was the special signal from the telephone switchboard if the director general or the controller wished to speak to a member of staff. Three sharp rings meant Sir John Reith, and two stood for Admiral Carpendale [his deputy]; on hearing the warning sounds the right technique was to pick up your phone

and say smartly, 'Yes, Sir!' I was told that Roger Eckersley, Director of Programmes, was in his office one afternoon when the phone gave four sharp rings. He looked apprehensively at his secretary. 'That must be God,' he said.

Reith maintained a belief in the concept of public-service broadcasting from the word go, and even the schedule published in the first issue of the *Radio Times* on 28 September 1923 demonstrates his conviction that listeners should be exposed to what was good for them:

A Recent Talk Broadcast from 2LO: *Photographing Wild Animals*, 5.00 *Woman's Hour-Ariel's Society Gossip*, Mrs C. S. Peel's *Kitchen Conversation*. 5.30 Children's Stories – *Little Black Sambo* by Katherine Bannerman, 6.15 *Boy's Brigade and Boy's Life Brigade News*. 6.25–7.00 Interval. 7.00 Time Signal, *First General News Bulletin*. 7.15 *Weekly Book Talk* by Mr John Strachey. 7.30 Symphony Concert with Augmented Orchestra, 9.10 Major General Sir William Sefton Brancker, Director of Civil Aviation, Air Ministry, on *The Possibility of Low Powered Aeroplanes*, 9.30 Time Signal, *Second General News Bulletin*. 9.40 Miss Daisy Kennedy Solo Violin, 10.30, close down.

In its emphasis on 'talks' of various types, the schedule anticipates a prominent feature of early television: the BBC talk was something common to both media. This selection shows that the output was in general sober and constrained, but it seems that even tighter restraints were applied to news broadcasts.

The Newspapers Proprietors Association was fearful of the effect that radio news might have upon sales of newspapers, and persuaded the government to restrict broadcasts until after 7 p.m. The bulletins were prepared by Reuters and telephoned through to the BBC, always beginning with the words 'London calling the British Isles. This is the first news bulletin, copyright from Reuter, Press Association, Exchange Telegraph Company, and Central News.' It was not until February 1930 that the Corporation was allowed to produce its own copy; Edgar Holt was employed to write this and he gives an account of what this entailed:

There were certain snags about writing the bulletins, for before I arrived on the scene a formidable rule-book had been compiled giving precise instructions about what might or might not be mentioned in BBC news. These excluded many subjects that filled the big-circulation newspapers and obliged us to concentrate on the most sober and respectable news of the day, though the odd funny item was graciously allowed as a tail-piece. This limitation of news topics gave rise to a curious incident on Good Friday 18 April 1930. Our Easter arrangements for that year included a single ten-minute bulletin for Good Friday evening and since it was not expected that there would be much trouble over this bulletin the second sub-editor was on duty alone, with myself on the end of a telephone in case she got into difficulty. As it turned out, it was a particularly dull Good Friday, and without the help of any of the present-day reporters and overseas correspondents who can bump out the news bulletins on dead evenings, she was unable to find more than two or three news items that were not forbidden by our rule book. That was the moment when she should have consulted me. But being a headstrong girl she decided to act on her own. Feeling that it was useless to put out a bulletin with only two or three items, she scrapped it altogether. At the appointed time I turned on the radio and was horrified when Stuart Hibberd, the chief announcer, cheerfully informed the waiting world: 'There is absolutely no news tonight, and we will have a piano interlude instead.'

In the early days there was frequently either a shortage of news or a shortage of newscasters. Holt describes how on 13 June 1931 an engineer read the news.

Announcers were in short supply at Savoy Hill; there were only six of them for all programmes and news bulletins. I was on duty with one of the sub-editors, who was suffering from a sore throat. We got the first news bulletin ready and waited for the announcer to come and read it through before going on to the studio. This was the usual practice but it was not invariable, since an announcer might have little time to spare between closing some other programme and going to the studio from which he was to read the news; and when no one came we took the bulletin down to the studio, left it there and went back to our office. It was due to be read at 6.15. At 6.19 our phone went. The control room said that no one had started to read the news yet, and where was the announcer? I said that we would find him. A quick dash to the announcer's room. Nobody there. What should we do? At that time my stammer was still with me, and I know I could never have got through a news bulletin. Then what about my sub-editor? He, being something of a hypochondriac, protested that he could not read the news because of his throat. We looked in other offices, hoping to find someone who could read a news bulletin. No one in the *Children's Hour* office, no one in outside broadcasts, no one in programme planning, no one in talks. At 6.15 on a Saturday afternoon the sub-editor and I were the only members of the programme staff in the whole of the BBC building. And time was going on. I went along to the lift, to see if the announcer was at last appearing, and as I did so, a young control room engineer came clattering down the stone stairs. I clutched at a straw. 'Can you read the news?' I asked. He said he would try and I hurried him along to the studio, put him down in front of the microphone and hoped for the best. It was a brave try. Certainly he had no BBC accent and it was unfortunate that one of the news items contained a number of French names, which were rather beyond him. But at least he read the bulletin. The show had gone on. He had barely finished reading when the announcer appeared. It was John Snagge, who had mistaken his time for coming on duty; he had thought that his evening turn started at 6.35 p.m., but he should have been there at 6.15 p.m. I had just time to tell him what had happened when the telephone rang in the announcer's room. On the line was the formidable Admiral Carpendale (BBC Controller, second in command to Sir John Reith) and in no sunny mood. 'Who's that?' 'Snagge, sir.' 'Who read the news?' 'An engineer, sir.' 'Engineer! Who ought to have read it?' 'I should, sir.' 'Why didn't you?' 'I wasn't here, sir.' 'Where were you?' 'In the Coal Hole [the BBC's local pub], sir.' Collapse, as the old *Punch* jokes used to have it, of elderly admiral.

What did the general public make of the manifest strengths and occasional weaknesses of the fledgeling service they were offered by the BBC? The Corporation was anxious to elicit their opinions, offering cash prizes in competitions geared to monitoring their responses. An indication of what the listening experience was like at the introduction of the service is to be found in the *Radio Times* of 26 October 1923. Under the heading ' "An Exciting Sunday" – A Reader's True Story', the following tale is told:

Time 3 pm – Visitors arrive specially to hear a broadcast concert on the recently erected wireless outfit. 3.05 pm – Everyone comfortable and armed with headphones, silence reigns – but, alas through the headphones also. 3.07 pm – Anxious host arises and tinkers with the Crystal with great ceremony and professional touch. 3.10 – 'Yes, we have no music to-day.' Still undaunted, he hastily leaves the room, goes into the garden, despite the downpour of rain, and examines the aerial minutely. 3.20 pm – host showing evident signs of what is commonly known as 'the wind up'. 3.25 pm – As the last resource, he carefully scrutinises the earth wire fixed to the water pipe and feels he must act. Glorious inspiration! Ah! The earth wire needs water! Forthwith, he saturates the water tap and earth wire attached. How simple. 3.30 – returns to visitors, delighted with the scene that awaits him. Everyone happy, listening to the delightful organ recital which is in progress. He is warmly congratulated on his detection of the fault, and he proudly exclaims, 'Wonderful thing this wireless, when one understands it. Why, you know, all that was really necessary was the earth wire needed water.' 3.45 – first item of programme concludes. Announcer of BBC conveys his apologies to listeners for thirty minutes delay in commencing concert. Collapse of host.

This account demonstrates how friends were invited to share the experience of listening to a broadcast, in the same way that watching television was to become something of a social engagement in the late 1930s, when the first sets came into circulation.

Without doubt, for many people being huddled around the wireless was a defining experience of the war, but it was not just the big, set-piece speeches of the nation's leaders that riveted the public. The BBC's Home Service, established in 1939, kept them entranced with a wide range of popular programmes. Almost 40 per cent of the population regularly tuned into Tommy Handley's comic *tour de force, ITMA*. (The initials stood for *It's That Man Again*, the tag by which the *Daily Express* referred to Hitler.) Music also played an important part in entertaining the nation, not just in maintaining morale but also in sustaining the output of workers. In 1940 *Music While You Work* was introduced, its brief to play upbeat pieces of music at a constant rhythm, in the belief that this would make the men and women in the munitions factories more productive in the repetitive tasks they had to do. The programme was so successful that in 1941 the Minister for Labour, Ernest Bevin, requested that the BBC should introduce a companion piece, called *Workers' Playtime*. These broadcasts were made from the factories themselves and consisted of comic sketches and sentimental songs. Both programmes long outlived the war, surviving in the schedules until 1967 and 1961 respectively.

The wartime entertainment offered by the wireless was not entirely frivolous; many worthy projects were attempted. A fine example of one of these was undertaken in 1941, when the BBC was officially asked by the government to produce a tribute to our Soviet allies, and a radio version of Eisenstein's film *Alexander Nevsky* was transmitted. Prokofiev wrote the score, which was played by the BBC Symphony Orchestra, accompanied by both the BBC Chorus and BBC Theatre Chorus and directed by Adrian Boult. The poet Louis MacNeice adapted the text from Eisenstein's original screenplay and actors of the calibre of Robert Donat took leading roles. This ambitious piece was broadcast live on 9 December, two days after the bombing of Pearl Harbor.

Almost from its inception, working on the wireless was popular with the acting profession. James Grout sings the praises of not having to learn screeds of dialogue. 'I love doing radio, there is not so much work in all, you don't have to learn the lines, but at the same time you can work some magic sometimes, if you've got a good script. You can sit down a lot; now I'm getting on, I like to sit down.'

His reference to the magical quality that the wireless was sometimes able to conjure up is echoed by presenter David Hamilton: 'Radio was what I always loved best, because it is a one-to-one medium. There is a magic about radio, I think.'

Because of radio's popularity, jobs were generally over-subscribed and it could be hard to break into the small pool of regular employees. Maurice Denham recalls, 'It took me a year to get an audition for BBC Radio. I arrived with three books with different characters in them and the director who was auditioning me called down to the studio from the control box, "Will you bend down and pick up that newspaper and read the first paragraph." After all the things that I'd been working on and working on in preparation, the whole thing seemed to hang upon whether you could read a piece out of the paper.'

Leading actors were often brought in for individual shows, but the bulk of the artists were drawn from what became known as the Radio Rep. In common with television, many of the points of reference for radio were initially drawn from the theatre and the Radio Rep operated very much like a theatrical repertory company, in that a pool of performers were contracted over a sustained period and were cast according to the requirements of each play. Maria Charles remembers that a sense of hierarchy was evident. 'If you were in the BBC Rep you were sort of "Hail fellow well met!", but if you were a guest artiste you were sort of treated differently when you arrived.' Edward Jewesbury has very positive recollections of his employment there. 'I was in the Radio Rep and I loved it. You got the chance to do so many different things – semi-documentary kinds of things, lots of plays. It was a proper rep – you'd play a very nice part one week and the next week you'd just be shouting in the background.'

As for preparation, Richard Bebb recalls that 'Radio was always properly funded and therefore there was none of the frenetic cutting of corners that you found in television. They always had time. The average radio drama producer had to produce two plays a month and even *Saturday Night Theatre* was only a four-day engagement. They were not exactly overworked, everything was much more comfortable and considered.' However, working in a new medium is always bewildering. Miriam Karlin points out that drama schools provided no training at all in the technique of working on the wireless. 'Directors would tell you to get in close to mike, or talk across mike. The technique is very different now because microphones are so different, everything is three-dimensional. There was never any radio training at RADA, but now they do radio, they do television, they do everything. Then one learned everything by experience, and that really is the best way to learn, although it seemed very daunting at the time – one was learning in front of a very large audience.'

One of the best ways to learn is by observation, as Michael Kilgarriff explains: 'I remember watching Norman Shelley, and thinking, *I'm really going to learn something here*. I've had no training in radio other than observing. In the days of mono recording you could have two or three people standing either side of the microphone, whereas with stereo you can only stand on one side. Norman Shelley always used to hold his arm out with his fist clenched so that he could just touch the microphone, and that was precisely the right distance. I watched him doing a particular scene and I was a bit disappointed really, his performance seemed competent but nothing special. Until I heard it. Three or four weeks later I listened to it and then I realized what those old boys could do. So much more seemed to be coming out of the speaker then he seemed to be putting in. It was something to do with taking your pauses. You would think on radio because there is no picture that you should be a bit quicker, but in fact they used to take it at a very steady pace and if anything pauses might even be longer. Providing you have the knack of doing it the right way, it could be tremendously exciting because every time there was one of these pauses, people would be thinking, *What's happening, what's going on, what's going on, what's he doing, what's he thinking?*, and it really kept them hooked.'

Since performers new to the wireless were obliged to learn the craft of radio acting as they went along – watching their peers and taking advice from whoever was kind enough to offer help – the experience must have been close to that of working in early television, a medium for which there was also no formal training in the pioneering days. Indeed, Miriam Karlin feels that the experience of war contributed to its success: 'No one was blasé, no one took anything for granted, you were all in it together and there was an incredible feeling of being in a team. Nobody wanted anything to go wrong from their own point of view. I suppose there was a wartime feeling of carrying on.'

In the early days of radio the Corporation did not have the facility to record programmes and everything was broadcast live, but by 1951, when *The Archers* first came on air, this was no longer the case. 'In those days we recorded the whole episode on one big fifteen-minute disc in one go,' says Norman Painting. 'One or two of those discs do survive, but they can only be played on the sort of equipment they had in the fifties, which is now only to be found in museums. So if you made a mistake it was almost like a live broadcast. If it was a dreadful mistake then we had to do the whole episode again, so it was almost the same as being live.' Later on, when the recording of television programmes also became possible, there was a similar period of transition, during which shows were performed 'as live' in order to minimize the need for post-production intervention.

Painting acknowledges the disadvantage of working live: 'I had done five hundred broadcasts, most of them live, before I appeared in *The Archers*. The trouble with the live broadcasts was that, once you had said it, you'd said it, you couldn't correct it.' However there was also a drawback to recording: 'If you know that you can do it again, it takes away a certain immediacy.'

One of the consequences of broadcasting live in either television or radio was that timing the programme became of crucial importance, in order to keep to the published schedules. Paul Rogers remembers that 'The news was sacred. Nothing stood in the way of it, so shows which overran would be truncated.' A number of actors recall cuts being made during the transmission itself, including Barbara Lott: 'I remember doing one play on the radio and it got very slow – we'd never managed to time it properly – and during transmission the door opened and there was the director standing with a great cardboard sign saying cut to page so-and-so.' Geoffrey Bayldon calls to mind an occasion when the director could have done with a similar sign. 'I can remember doing a live radio broadcast. The play was directed by Peter Dews and had a sweet, naïve young girl in it who was doing her first ever broadcast. Peter Dews was sitting behind the producer's glass panel and he started circling his index finger, making "Speed up" signs. The girl had no idea, it was her first time; she glanced up, saw him, and did it back [repeated it] with a big smile on her face.'

Not having learned their lines by heart, artists were at the mercy of the words on the page. Barbara Lott recounts what happened to the distinguished actor Robert Donat: 'He was standing on one side of the mike holding his script and he'd taken out the pin that held the pages together. Suddenly, like a sheaf of cards, the whole thing slid on to the floor. Somebody standing the other side of the mike saw it begin to happen, and he dropped down on to his knees and collected it as it began to fall.'

The success of the Home Service throughout the war meant that with the arrival of peace the BBC was well placed to add two additional channels to its output. The Light Programme took to the air in 1945 and the Third Programme a year later. Under this tripartite system, the Home Service was envisaged as the base for speech radio and more serious scheduling, the Light for popular music and comedy and the Third for classical music and more weighty material. The onset of peace brought forth a rash of new programmes, many of which survive to the present day. *Letter From America* was first broadcast in March 1946, *Down Your Way* began in December that year, *Twenty Questions* joined the repertoire in February 1947 and *Round Britain Quiz* started in November 1947. The first Reith lecture was heard in October 1948 and *Listen With Mother* was introduced in October 1950. The legendary *Goon Show* first stormed the airwaves in 1951 and stalwarts the *Today* programme and *The World at One* commenced in 1957 and 1965 respectively.

Above all, the post-war era proved to be a golden age for radio comedy. Among many hit series was the vehicle for the comedian Ted Ray, *Ray's a Laugh*, which ran from 1949 to 1961. *Take It From Here* was launched in 1948 and survived until 1959, providing Frank Muir and Dennis Norden with their first break. *The Goon Show* ran for eight years, and another of the greatest successes of this period was *Much Binding in the Marsh* (1947–53), in which Maurice Denham starred with Richard Murdoch and Kenneth Horne.

Although the BBC excelled in the field of comedy at this time, they did not neglect serious drama. One of their flagship programmes was *Saturday Night Theatre*, and Richard Bebb remembers how well-regarded this was within the acting profession: 'If you did *Saturday Night Theatre* there were ten million listeners. It was a tremendously important outlet for actors.' Bebb also featured in one of the greatest drama productions undertaken by the Corporation during the early 1950s: 'The very first thing I did when I joined the Radio Rep was to co-narrate *Under Milk Wood*.' The production was a huge critical and commercial success and had a great impact on those who listened to the initial broadcast, amongst them Richard Digby Day: 'I come from a generation that was entirely brought up on radio. I can still vividly remember my mother making us sit down to listen to the first broadcast of *Under Milk Wood*. I've absolutely never forgotten the profound impression it made on me.'

The conclusion of the war signalled that radio's monopoly over the British public would soon be broken, as plans were under way to take the television service out of mothballs. Since they functioned as separate and competitive parts of the Corporation, the two media quickly became rivals. 'I started in the war in about 1943 and radio really was the thing,' says Barbara Lott. 'Then suddenly the war ended and television restarted. I started to be offered work in television and (a), the money was better, and (b), it was exciting, so I began to do rather a lot. Then I remember a radio producer ringing up and offering me two days' work about five weeks ahead, and my agent must have said that she couldn't commit me that far ahead in case a television came up. He [the producer] telephoned me and said, "I think you've got to make your mind up, Barbara: are you going to do television or radio? You can't do both." I said, "I want to do both. I've never wanted to be part of one medium." He never employed me again. There was real rivalry, real rivalry between Broadcasting House and Alexandra Palace.'

3

Television in the Post-war Period 1946–55

AFTER FOUR YEARS of war, Allied troops entered Messina in the autumn of 1943 and soon afterwawrds the Italians signed an armistice with them. On the eastern front, the Russian Army had taken Kiev. These events must have been a boost to morale at home in England and it is perhaps no coincidence that this was the month in which the government took the optimistic decision to establish a committee to consider the nature and development of television broadcasting once the conflict was over.

In the event, transmissions did not resume until 7 June 1946, when Jasmine Bligh, who had worked as a presenter on the fledgeling service before the war, spoke directly to camera outside Alexandra Palace, saying, 'Hello, remember me?' The last programme shown before the service was suspended had been a Mickey Mouse cartoon, and in a nod to continuity the BBC was careful to include the same cartoon among the programmes for the day of the relaunch. Other things remained the same as well – there had been little research and development in the intervening years and many technological capabilities had not advanced, in particular the distance that transmissions were able to travel, which remained within a radius of approximately forty miles from Alexandra Palace.

In a bid to raise funds so that the service could progress and improve, in 1946 the BBC introduced a combined radio and television licence, which cost £2. With the additional money they were able to build a second transmitter at Birmingham, thus making television available to a much wider potential audience in the Midlands and the North. And they needed all the funding they could lay their hands on, because the film industry, the West End theatre managements and many sporting organisations, concerned at the threat to their own audiences by the growth of this new medium, continued their pre-war refusal to co-operate with the BBC. This meant that the Corporation was unable to bulk out the schedules with motion pictures and sporting fixtures – they were not even allowed to transmit newsreels. Everything that was shown on the service had to be home-grown, and this proved to be a costly business. It also explains why live television at this time was so prolific, for by 1954 BBC TV was broadcasting for six hours a day, seven days a week.

When broadcasts restarted in 1946 it is estimated that roughly fifteen thousand households watched the service. Within two years this figure had increased to fifty-four thousand, and by 1949 it had topped ninety thousand. During this period the BBC achieved a number of coups. Within twenty hours of reopening for business it was able to show the Victory Parade, but this achievement paled into insignificance compared to its success in televising the

1948 Olympic Games, which were held in London. The Corporation was able to bring action from twenty-five different venues to the small screen, and without doubt this helped to increase confidence in and enthusiasm for the new medium.

This increase in outside broadcasting partly stemmed from necessity, since it was becoming apparent that the two pre-war studios at Alexandra Palace were inadequate for the greater demands now being made on them. Accordingly, in 1949 the BBC obtained a lease on some studios in Lime Grove, which they regarded as a mid-term solution to the problem. In the meantime they were given permission by the London County Council to prepare plans for a purpose-built television centre to be constructed at White City.

Venetia Barrett describes the BBC's interim accommodation: 'The studios at Lime Grove looked like an ordinary house from the outside – the front might have been slightly modernised, but not much.' Ian Carmichael remembers the welcome sense of relief after the confines of Ally Pally: 'I was in a show that opened Studio D in the new Lime Grove building. It was heaven in comparison with what we'd had at Alexandra Palace. It was three times the size and Eric Robinson and the orchestra got a studio all of their own.' Miriam Karlin agrees that 'Lime Grove was quite luxurious compared to Alexandra Palace,' but other actors have mixed feelings about television's new quarters. 'At Lime Grove when we did things you didn't get into the studio until the eleventh hour,' recalled Nigel Hawthorne. 'You rehearsed in some boys' club somewhere, which never had any heating, then you were dragged into the studio and thrown on to a set which you'd never seen in your life before and told to get on with it. You didn't get any really satisfactory preparation. There was very much the feeling that people were learning things as they went along.' In contrast to this, James Grout detected marked progress: 'In Lime Grove the whole process had got much more slick. You knew who people were. When I first started you didn't know who anybody was except possibly the director. But in Lime Grove everyone had a position and you knew what that position was and how to react to it.'

Although the move to Lime Grove must have represented a milestone for those working in television, for members of the public the real turning point came with the Queen's coronation in 1953. More than twenty million people throughout the country witnessed a marathon account of the ceremony lasting from ten-fifteen in the morning until five-twenty in the afternoon, sharing the occasion with neighbours and friends at home, or watching it in shops, halls, even churches. One actor recalled seeing the event with a large group of people, amongst whom was a retired soldier who considered it would be disrespectful to sit while the sovereign was being crowned, and stood to attention at the back of the room for the duration of the service. A member of the public, Anne Godfrey, has a childhood memory of watching the ceremony on television through a large perspex screen which was stood in front of the set in order to magnify the tiny picture so that as many people as possible could get a decent view. The actress Eve Pearce also remembers seeing the great occasion: 'The first time I saw television was in my rep days and it was the coronation. The board of the theatre hired one specially. We did a special matinée for the coronation, so we could only see bits of it. They put it in the green-room and every time you came off stage you dashed to see a bit of it. We thought it was wonderful. There was a great sense of excitement – what would one see?'

The television historian Andrew Crisell sums up the importance of this moment: 'The coronation usefully symbolises the point where television surpassed radio as the major mass medium. In itself it prompted a boom in the sales of TV sets, and 1953 was the first year in which more television than radio sets were manufactured, at an average unit price of about £85.' The sudden expansion of the TV audience would make a difference to the acting profession. Peter Byrne, who played Sergeant Crawford in *Dixon of Dock Green* for more than twenty-three years, recalls, 'I started back in 1953. Because of the coronation people had just bought their sets on the HP. It was a novelty so they tended to watch the thing from the test card in the morning until the dot at night. Everybody had nine-inch oblong eyeballs.'

In spite of the triumph of the coronation, television was still very much the junior partner at the BBC, where the powers that be, ensconced in radio's headquarters in central London, viewed the young pretender at Alexandra Palace with profound misgivings. In fact, in 1950 the entire television budget amounted to only half the sum allocated to the Home Service alone on radio, which clearly demonstrates the priorities within the Corporation. Richard Bebb, who worked as an actor in both television and radio at that time, explains: 'In 1950 the whole of television was run from Broadcasting House by people who hated television. Every administrative job – head of drama, head of variety – was filled by people from Broadcasting House. They wanted to keep their hands on television and to starve it. Then in November 1952 or 1953 there was a complete palace revolution and everyone from Broadcasting House was thrown out and the major jobs were offered to television people. All the directors I'd been working for were offered jobs in administration that they felt they couldn't refuse. Michael Barry became Head of Drama; Royston Morley became head of the newly created television school, to teach trainee television directors.' (In fact it is likely that the revolution Bebb mentions occurred slightly earlier, as in 1950 the Controller of Television, Norman Collins, became so frustrated by the hostility he faced within the Corporation that he resigned, triggering a number of changes in the administration.)

Perhaps because of this rivalry between the two domains, very few staff moved from working on the wireless to television. A large proportion of the producers, directors, technicians and performers employed during the days when television was broadcast live were poached directly from the theatre. Colin Welland explains that 'In those days television acting was an extension of stage acting, except it was more intimate. Although you had an audience of millions, you had to think of it in terms of playing to two or three people in a small room.' The actor Harry Landis makes the point that 'The honesty, sincerity and feeling are the same whether it's film, television or theatre.' However, the challenge for many television pioneers was to develop skills tailored to the new medium, which they did by trial and error. 'Moving into the new medium of television from the stage, we pitched our performances more by luck than judgement,' says Roger Ostime. 'When I was at RADA from 1949 to 1951 there was no training for television at all, so you really had to use your common sense.'

Ostime's wife, actress Hilary Mason, found that her colleagues could be a source of inspiration. 'In the beginning I felt a bit lost, but I just watched the other actors. Because it was live you couldn't even watch yourself and pick up your mistakes that way. Once I'd done it, I really did take to it like a duck to water, I loved it.' Ian Flintoff found it quite easy to adapt: 'I don't think actors were histrionic on television – even if they could have filled the stage of the Olivier Theatre they didn't bring that quality to the studio with them. Everyone has the ordinary everyday experience of simply talking to their friends and that kind of experience is there for actors to draw on.' Despite the actors' lack of experience, they seem to have received little, if any, directorial assistance. Maria Charles states, 'I was never aware of when I was going to be in close-up, I don't even remember there being a light on the camera. Now, of course, you know.' Stephen Hancock was equally baffled. 'Often you didn't know what camera was on you, or what lens was on you, or whether it was long shot or close-up. If you were in close-up you could raise your eyebrow by one centimetre and it spoke volumes, but if you were in long shot you would have to do something a bit bigger.' He eventually devised a solution to this problem. 'In the end I used to get the PA [production assistant] to give me a camera script so that I could work out which camera was on me at which time. There wasn't time for the director to say, "You're doing too much."'

Others were more fortunate: Barbara Lott recalls being offered specific advice. 'You were given a lot of instructions as to how not to act by the director. One was told to underplay, rightly, and not to make big gestures. There was an awareness that it was all different. People who had done a lot of filming had an easier time of it; they understood the understatement.' Paul Rogers appears to have taken the transition in his stride: 'Working on television wasn't a strain, it wasn't a shock, but it did employ a certain awareness of the camera. You didn't play to it but you were aware of it. I probably enjoyed the most wonderful time of freedom in television acting. There was something very thrilling about being involved in such a splendidly oiled piece of machinery. You had three or maybe four cameras, like Daleks. There was a jolly good way of making sure you were in shot: you had to be able to see the lens.'

But for Maurice Denham it was perturbing: 'I had done three years of weekly rep and was very much stage-bound; my projection was far too much for television. That was a shock; you had to take it down and down and down so that it became more or less natural.' And for Malcolm Farquhar it was clearly traumatic. 'We were told we could not do what we did on the stage. I think that made us rather inhibited and we gave rather dull performances. It wasn't until later when you found the technique – actors now are so good on telly and they're not very good on the stage. I always felt that I was not very good on telly, I felt harnessed. I wasn't asked very often to do it! When we were told not to pull faces we were insulted. I remember thinking, *They don't know what they're talking about. They don't know what great acting is, making me come down to this!* It was completely foreign to everyone.'

Bernard Hepton also expresses a sense of bewilderment: 'Coming from the theatre, actors were not used to the proximity of the microphone and the proximity of the camera and we were told, "Don't act, behave." I couldn't understand what they were talking about – not a lot of people could in those early days – but the microphone actually brought the voices down because they were too loud and the camera meant that you played to an audience who were six feet away from you. This took a lot of getting used to.' An example of the kind of technical problem actors had to overcome is provided by Judy Campbell: 'We all had to learn the things you mustn't do, like leaning forward and saying, "Would you like a cigarette?" because your head would blot out the screen.'

In order to engage with the subtleties of television acting, performers had first to get a job. This could be achieved in a variety of ways, and Paul Williamson suggests that it was rarely accomplished by means of an audition. 'I don't ever remember being auditioned or interviewed for jobs. If directors wanted you they phoned your agent. Good agents were trusted. Casting directors were only used for films in those days.' Denied the more conventional route of job interviews, artists were often obliged to make use of personal contacts. Nigel Hawthorne remembered, 'I had known [director] Shaun Sutton from when I began as an actor in 1950 in Cape Town. When I came to England he met me at Waterloo and it was really through him that I got up to Buxton Rep. Shaun drifted into television, where he joined the children's section.' Hawthorne's track record with Sutton enabled him to start working in children's television too, initially in a programme called *Hurrah for Halloween*, starring Joan Sims.

Presenter Adrian Cairns discovered an ingenious method of getting his foot in the door. 'These were the days of *Café Continental* [a revue show which ran from 1947 to 1953]. There was a studio at Alexandra Palace and if you brought your own dinner jacket with you, you got £7 per night to go along and react to the variety acts that were performing.' A similar ploy was used by Brian Murphy: 'I did a lot of work as a featured extra in the early days [1956–7] because someone suggested it was a good means to find your way around this new medium. I think we were paid about £3 a day. I was warned by more experienced actors not to show my face too much, just to hover in the background, firstly because it meant you couldn't be used again, but secondly so that you didn't become too established as a walk-on artist if you had ambitions to become more than that. So you lurked.'

Venetia Barrett is able to give a broad picture of the kind of remuneration for a typical week's work. 'I did a thirty-minute play in 1950. We rehearsed in the Goat and Compasses, Euston Road, near Warren Street tube. I was paid ten guineas for the whole thing, which was quite a lot then.' For a single appearance in the country's first ever television soap, *The Grove Family*, 'The episode only ran for quarter of an hour, for which there were seven days' rehearsal. I was paid seven guineas' rehearsal fee and six guineas for the performance.'

Peter Bowles explains the BBC's old-fashioned methods: 'You were paid in guineas by the BBC. If you worked for the BBC you were really supposed to be a gentleman – it echoes that thing of the newsreaders having to wear a dinner jacket even if they were on the radio.' Not content with paying in this out-moded way, the corporation also devised an extremely complicated salary scale. 'To pay you the BBC had these terrible categories,' says George Baker. 'The play was designated Cat A, Cat B, Cat C, and all your fees stemmed from the fees they decided to pay you for your Cat C. So if you got £50 for your Cat C, you might get £150 for a Cat A. Within this system, they used to have these things called "special high".' Eve Pearce remembers the opposite of the 'special high': 'They even had something called a "special low". If you did anything remotely religious you got a "special low", because religious programmes never had any money. I remember one year I did a series of four programmes on the four saint's days – I was doing the one about St Patrick, with George Baker as St Patrick. You didn't know St Patrick had a sister, did you? Well, he did in this. That was a very "special low" because it was about St Patrick.' The general feeling is that the level of pay was unimpressive, as Nigel Hawthorne said: 'I don't think I got very much money but the experience of it was so extraordinary that you did it for that.'

An indication of how television fees compared unfavourably to the salaries paid in repertory companies is given by Richard Bebb: 'For *Promise of Tomorrow* we rehearsed for a month and gave two performances – one on the Sunday and the repeat the following Thursday. In effect it was five weeks' work, for which I was paid £28. In a sense the pay was less good than in rep – I was paid £8 a week in Buxton the year before.'

The BBC kept a close eye on its costs, and so the amount of time allotted for rehearsal usually depended on the length of the play in question. However, TV usually needed more rehearsal time than theatre. 'We had four weeks' rehearsal in those days, I kid you not. You had to know it as for the theatre because you were doing it live,' says Miriam Karlin. 'We had about a fortnight or three weeks' rehearsal, far more than we got for weekly rep,' recalled Maurice Denham. 'There was the added thing of the absolute position you had to be in for any particular line – if you weren't there the camera couldn't get you.' James Grout also emphasizes the need to be accurate for the cameras: 'Not many people realise the exactitude that is necessary for successful telly. The vision mixer will cut from one camera to another on a word cue given by the actor in the course of a scene. If the actor gets the word wrong, that really buggers it up.' 'Almost everything was rehearsed at 35 Marylebone High Street. This was the *Radio Times* shop and above the shop were the offices of the editorial people. At the back the BBC bought a very large series of outbuildings. They formed about five rooms along a corridor and that's where all the rehearsing was done,' recalls Richard Bebb.

In order to guarantee the best level of accuracy, a special camera rehearsal was held to ensure that the transition to studio was as seamless as possible. Even so, according to Bebb, things did not necessarily run smoothly. 'However good you were technically and however good the director was technically, when it came to shooting with two or three cameras there had to be certain adaptations from what you'd established at rehearsal. You had at the last moment to make an enormous number of adjustments. There wasn't enough studio time and that was a problem.' Ian Carmichael also complains about the brevity of camera-rehearsal time: 'Camera time was absolutely minimal. These shows were about an hour and a half long but you never got to rehearse with cameras until ten-thirty on the morning of transmission, so all the camera rehearsals were done under tremendous pressure. You just had to press on.'

Leonard Lewis worked as a director on many episodes of *Z Cars*: 'When you went into the first morning of the camera rehearsal you went through the show piece by piece. There was at least one director who used to do a run-through of the whole show and that was quite fun. It used to be quite a hesitant, jerky run-through but it did give everybody in the studio some idea of what the whole thing would be like. If you were very lucky, at the end of the first day you might be in a state where you could do a run-through, but usually speaking you wouldn't do a run-through until the next day. Ideally, by the morning of the second day you did a staggered, stopping and starting run-through and then at about half-past four or five o'clock you did a dress run-through, which was as polished as it was going to be – you hoped.'

An extended period of rehearsal has benefits for an actor too: 'If you're dropped at the deep end on the first day, there are a lot of nuances you can't get hold of, but if you have a rehearsal period then some of that becomes possible,' says Brian Murphy. 'You can use the time to nurture the performance and dig into the script. There is a voyage of discovery. As an actor that is something that I miss now because I think it's the creative process and you can't skip it. That's something the people who run the business these days can't understand because it doesn't make money, so they don't totally understand it . . . it's not somebody's perverse idea to waste time.'

Far from wasting time, proper rehearsal can avoid the kind of accident that Malcolm Farquhar once witnessed. 'I did something called *Star and Company* at the Riverside Studios. It was an early soap, on for four or five nights a week. There was a scene in it when they were moving house, they were clearing a room. The furniture went out, the rolled-up carpets and everything, and we were left behind. I thought, *Surely somebody is going to rehearse this?* but nothing happened – there was only three days' rehearsal for each episode. They just mimed it – "You do this, you do this, you do that." I went to the director and said, "We must rehearse this, you know. How do we know how long it is going to take to get the stuff out through the door? We've got to roll the carpet up and I don't think we've got enough dialogue." He said, "Oh rubbish, we haven't got time for that sort of thing." We went live on it and they started clearing stuff out. What dialogue the audience heard I don't know, because there was so much noise. The last thing to go was the carpet and the actor turned round with it on his shoulder and knocked one of the others flying, knocked him out.'

There were many bizarre challenges for the actors doing live television. Janet Hargreaves remembers a particular episode of *Compact*: 'It was Shrove Tuesday and according to the storyline my character had to make pancakes, and I had to toss them. The pan was steaming and smoking away, but I did manage to catch them.' Actors had to rely on their ingenuity as well as their dexterity. For *The Passionate Pilgrim*, about the Crimean War, James Grout recalls, 'There were about six of us lads, and we formed the entire British Army. We had to return from battle during a love scene between Andrew Osborne and Jill Balcon that went on for about twenty minutes. Michael Barry was the director and he had this idea that he wanted us to return from battle all bashed up, and he did it with shadows. He threw the shadows against the back wall while the principal actors were acting away in the front, properly lit. You started from behind the camera, then you'd go round in front of the light which threw the shadow on the back wall; you were in that light for about two or three paces, then you had to hare like a madman for about thirty yards round the back of the set and hope to goodness that you got back in time as the last person was going across the light so that you could follow on again. Every time you walked across the light you had to try and throw a different shadow, so for twenty minutes they had this wonderful procession of six actors rushing round like maniacs then adopting some strange . . . pose. Of course, we all tried to outdo each other.'

One of the most daunting prospects for an actor is being asked to sing if he is not really confident of his voice. George Baker played the composer Percy French in *The Last Troubadour*, 'and when it was offered to me I said, "I can't sing." You must understand that I am simply unable to sing. They said to me, "Don't worry about that, don't worry about that, it's just the story." And when I got the script it was indeed just the story, but it was too short, so they decided that yes, I could sing. It was trauma. The producer was a purist and he said, "He used to accompany himself on a banjo." Well, I can't sing and I certainly can't play the banjo. They said, "It's perfectly all right, we'll get somebody else to play the banjo." So, Percy's wife dies . . . It's a long crane shot and I'm looking down on the wife and beginning to sing and your man with the banjo is standing there and as the crane moves, he moves – he has to because otherwise he would have been caught on camera. The first couple of notes were all right but then for all the rest I couldn't hear a single one, not a single note. To add to everything, they had not had the songs reset and there was a little shut-eye note right at the top at the end. There was a lovely man in the programme called Paddy Joyce, and as I went across to go to the next set – with three dressers helping me to do a costume change on the run – I said to Paddy, "Did I hit it?" And he said, "Well, let's say you wounded it!" '

Faced with difficulties such as these, actors are often obliged to rely upon technique to carry them through, but it took a while to develop an awareness of the kind of craft that was appropriate and effective. Judy Campbell explains the complexity of what could be demanded of a performer: 'The whole thing was technically very complicated because you had to come to certain marks. I remember in one play – heaven knows what it was – I was to have a close-up at one point. There was a mantelpiece with the usual ornaments on it and a clock in the middle. We played the scene using the camera that was facing the fireplace, then one faced away and played another scene opposite, during which time they moved the clock and in a hole in the scenery a camera poked its nose through to take a close-up of me. I in the meantime had had to move to a very exact mark on the floor, because if I had been a few inches to the left or a few inches to the right I wouldn't have got my close-up. If you could do that, and give a performance, and cry at the right time or whatever it was, and bring it in on time, you were really rather pleased with yourself. It was like riding in a race, where you've got to be very careful and very precise, yet at the same time go at a good speed and take some fences on the way. That's what it felt like.'

A number of artists relished the fact that once the transmission was in progress there was little anyone could do to influence their work. Barbara Lott was one of several who spoke of the feeling of being in control: 'In live television you have more control over your performance than you do in recorded television or film, particularly if you're playing an emotional part. You would suddenly think, *I'm not going to do that way, I'm going to play it much quieter*, or, *I don't think I'm going to be so violent.* If you're filming and you do that – "What do you think you're doing, Barbara?" But in live television you are in control, just as you are in the theatre. I think possibly that's why so many people came from the theatre into television, rather than from film.'

Peter Byrne concurs: 'In live television you are much more in control of your performance than you are today. In a live performance, particularly if you knew the vision mixer, you could wait out that dangerous pause. You knew that it was working and that the vision mixer would wait and not cut away – there's no point in working your socks of if you're out of shot.' Harry Landis points out that 'On film or recorded television, if an editor decides you will answer a question one second before you felt it was right, for their own reason, they can snip out that much tape to get the reply quicker. Your rhythm doesn't exist, their rhythm makes the programme.'

Christopher Lee has learned to be wary of the power of the editor to make the kind of alterations that Landis describes. 'The only time I like live television – prefer it – is when I'm being interviewed, because they can't do anything to my answers. If you're doing a talk show and it's taped, they can and do distort your answers to an extent where you end up saying yes when you actually said no, by cutting the tape. I distrust taped television interviews enormously.'

As a presenter with the fledgeling ITV station Tyne Tees, Adrian Cairns regularly found himself on the other end of the interviewing sofa, and recalls being thrown in at the deep end. 'I started by interviewing the Prime Minister, Harold Macmillan, on the opening night. The Managing Director said to me, "You are interviewing the Prime Minister, Adrian. Don't ask him anything political. Find out what he had for breakfast." I had eight minutes, which is quite a long time for an interview. His Parliamentary Private Secretary enquired what I was going to ask and suggested that I get him talking about Stockton [his constituency]. Macmillan was marvellous, he made it so easy. The interviewer was subservient to politicians in those days. I was placed on a chair much lower than the one Macmillan sat on, I was almost crouching down, looking up at him.'

Newsreading was also harder than it looked. 'In those days we didn't have autocue or teleprompt,' says Bob

Holness, 'you had to read the news on a remote-controlled camera in a sort of cupboard-like room. You'd go in, sit down, place yourself right and you'd be told exactly what time you were starting. This remote-controlled camera would zoom in and out and you would talk to it. You couldn't see anybody else about, you couldn't see anyone in the control room. You were completely boxed in. The instructions as you went in were "Don't forget to look up every second line." To be sure that you were talking to the audience, you absorbed two lines and then looked up, absorbed another two lines and looked up. I suppose it was fairly pedantic and pedestrian in those days, it looked as though you were reading. It was fairly nerve-racking but it was a good discipline. You had to keep one eye on the clock, one eye on the camera and a third eye looking down at your script. If a bit of late news came in, the door very softly opened and a piece of paper would appear in front of you and you had no idea what was on it.'

Colin Welland however feels that the autocue has not improved presentation: 'We had to work from the script, you had to present *yourself* to the audience. Nowadays you have a lot of glassy-eyed presenters, and television has become glib.' When so much of the work in live television was unpredictable, there was little chance of presenters becoming glassy-eyed. Tom Edwards was not alone in finding that he was regularly faced with the unexpected. 'I sometimes had to sight-read news bulletins, if the news was coming in late. There was a notorious news editor at Broadcasting House who was fond of the strong stuff and if he was on duty the bulletin would arrive only just in time. Sometimes I'd receive a script with the first page of the bulletin and page 2 hadn't yet arrived and I'd have to sight-read it, which got the old adrenalin going. If I was sight-reading and I got a place name wrong or mispronounced something, my boss was furious. I remember once having to ad-lib to camera for about four minutes. The telecine machine to show film for the newscast broke down and almost all the items for that programme were on film. The director told me through the floor manager, "Tom, you're just going to have to give us a guided tour of the studio." They gave me a stick microphone and I went round saying, "This is Joe Bloggs on camera one, this is So-and-so, this is So-and-so." That's how I learned my craft as a broadcaster – by my mistakes and by things going wrong.'

Even if all the equipment remained in working order, Ian Flintoff recalls that the presenters were constantly kept on their toes. 'On one occasion a six-minute film came in at the last moment without my having a chance to see it. The film was divided up into about ten little stories and I hadn't a clue what any of them were about. I had the script in front of me and I was watching what was on the screen and I had to synchronize the commentary with what I could see. I didn't want to be talking about a Rolls-Royce motor car when there was a flock of sheep on the screen. When I got to the end of that six minutes I could hear a huge whoop of delight from the control box.' In spite of these ordeals, Flintoff remains dismissive about the demands of the work. 'I think it's one of the easiest jobs in the world. I think there's a great deal of mystique about it. You need integrity, you need to be there on time and know what's going to come up on the news.'

Many artists had to struggle to maintain a grip on their

fear, haunted by the prospect of making a mistake in front of millions of people. 'I suppose it's to do with mathematics, but if you make a mistake or fluff a line on camera, it's multiplied by several million compared to forgetting a line on stage,' says Ian Flintoff. James Grout confesses, 'It was terrifying, absolutely terrifying, much worse than theatre,' and Stephen Hancock identifies the point at which the fear kicked in: 'They had a little light halfway up the wall and it kept flashing, "Standby, standby," then suddenly it went red and it said, "On air, on air." That was the most terrifying moment.' Glyn Houston is in agreement: 'When that red light goes on, it doesn't matter if it's recorded or live, actors are nervous.' Miriam Karlin recalls her response to this: 'There was a countdown until the moment when you start and that really was a scary feeling. That moment you thought, *I'm sure I should have peed.*'

For others, nerves took physical toll. Margaret Tyzack says, 'I remember always the sweating horror of it. I never used to throw up before the transmission, I used to throw up when we had finished.' On some occasions the poor terrified performers were unable even to wait until the end of the show to throw up, according to Eve Pearce: 'There was an actor called Hugh David who used to do a series called *Knight Errant*. He was acting with a girl who wasn't experienced at all and she was terribly, terribly nervous. Suddenly in the middle of the scene she disappeared, leaving him alone on the screen, and he could hear her being sick behind a flat [fake wall], so he had to make up this huge speech.' Mary Kenton recalls another example of the terror that afflicted some unfortunates. 'When I was working at Alexandra Palace, I remember how frightening it was. Somebody told me that two weeks before, they were doing *The Merchant of Venice* and the man who was playing the Prince of Morocco came on, said, "Lady, mislike me not for my complexion," and fainted dead away. The cameraman didn't know what to do, so they cut to that standby film of a kitten playing with a ball of wool.'

Richard O'Callaghan mentions another effect that stage-fright can have on a performer: '*Z Cars* went on being live long after anything else did . . . There was a middle-aged man playing a doctor and it became obvious that he hadn't a clue what he was supposed to be saying. He'd gone into a complete and utter panic. Behind him was Frank Windsor, who'd gone sort of green on a black and white television. The man went to a telephone which wasn't ringing and picked it up and said, "Hello? Hello?" The sound went dead but he apparently carried on gibbering, then the sound came back and you could hear him being given his cue. This went on, and on, and on. It completely horrified me. It was like watching somebody being murdered.' He was due to be on the show himself, and 'I could see me in three weeks' time being in the same situation. I felt so upset for him, terrified for myself. When I got to the rehearsals they were absolutely crazy. Every single member of the cast except Stratford Johns was carrying three or four water pistols. There were squirts of water shooting all over the place – they'd gone completely nuts . . . The director only seemed to want to rehearse until about midday, then he'd say, "Let's go across to Kew Gardens for the afternoon." I got lulled into this very false sense of security . . . We had two days rehearsing in the studio with the live transmission on the evening of the second day. So there we were with half-cars that we had to get bundled into and cameras rushing about from one place to another. The first day was fine and the second day was fine until the late afternoon, early evening, when they sent us all off for supper. I ate far too much of all the wrong kind of food, got back into make-up and suddenly this appalling attack of fear hit me and it got worse and worse and worse. I couldn't understand what anybody was saying to me; I was in a complete state of panic. I went down to the studio and came across other members of the cast sitting locked into themselves. They said that even after four years when it came to this point they wished they'd never ever agreed to do it. There was this bunch of completely terrified people waiting for the show to start with the clock ticking away. Eventually you'd get a voice saying, "Come on, everybody get ready, we've got ten seconds." I stood waiting and waiting, then we got a "Go!" And I suddenly thought, *What's my next line? I don't know what my next line is.* And I sat there, totally without a clue, and as I was thinking it suddenly came out and the relief was just fantastic. From then on I felt OK and in fact I became quite excited. There was no room for any kind of mistake at all. It was incredibly slick and professional.'

A number of artists observed that the stress of live performance was so great that many people turned to drink to help them cope with it. Wendy Craig says, 'When you finished doing a live television, it had been so frightening, so dreadful, that people used to rush to the bar and order large brandies to recover. The terror of forgetting your lines live on camera – it was a nightmare.' Stephen Hancock remembers, 'After doing a live show the relief was so great that you almost went into shock. You'd have to get to the bar and sink half a pint or so before you were human again.' According to Harry Landis, some did not wait until the end of the show to start drinking. 'I did an episode of *No Hiding Place* where the actor playing my brother was an alcoholic. At the dress rehearsal he was still reading it from the script and we were going out live in an hour. I was terrified because all my stuff was with him live. He went up to the bar and had twelve double Scotches and he was perfect. I was the one that was stammering with terror, but once he'd settled his nerves with the drink he was fine.'

In 1954 Paul Rogers won a Best Actor award for his role in *The Three Sisters*, an achievement that is magnified in light of the following confession: 'The dreadful thing about those early productions was that you did a repeat. You did a performance on Sunday night and then another on Thursday. You left the performance for three days and then all you had was a run-through before the second showing; it meant the nerves were appalling. Rosalie [Crutchley] arrived on Thursday and said, "Darlings, I've got the answer. No more nerves. Oblovon. It's marvellous. We take it fifteen minutes before." There it was, a perfectly legitimate chemist's drug. I remember they looked like rather large jewels. We popped them in our mouths, certain it would be a great relief, and it was. I had absolutely not a shred of nerves. It wasn't until I realized they put the cut key in for the third time [i.e. cut off the sound to simulate a technical breakdown, rather than transmit the actors' words] . . . I dried terribly happily, couldn't care less, it was marvellous, then suddenly something inside me said, *What the hell do you think you're doing?* From then on I was fine, absolutely fine.' Josephine Tewson explains the use of the 'cut key', which was wielded by the prompter. 'In those days if actors dried they would press a little button that cut the sound out, give them the line and then let the button go. So if you were watching at home all you would think was, *Oh, the sound's gone on my television!* And suddenly it would be back again.'

Not every programme had the cut-key facility, and Geoffrey Bayldon describes being left high and dry without it. 'In Birmingham I did *The Case of the Frightened Lady*. I was the murderer, killing women by strangling them with scarves. During the last scene when I was confronted by the inspector, I had to bring out the handkerchief I had used in the killings. I looked down at it and dried completely. The camera was coming in closer. The prompt, when it came, was terribly gabbled – the stage manager didn't have the cut key and so she spoke it very quickly, but the whole of Britain heard it. Having thought I was going to be all right, I dried again. In the end the inspector hissed, "Scarf!!!" at me and I was able to go on. A few seconds later my character had to pull out a gun and shoot himself, which I did with an *enormous* amount of relief.'

However, Barbara Lott preferred not to use the cut key: 'Using the cut key was terrible. If you dried they pressed the cut key and a little ASM would wriggle her way towards you on her hands and knees or even her tummy and you'd hear a voice coming up from your feet giving you your line. It was much better really just to press on and hope for the best.' The system was by no means failsafe and often caused more problems than it solved, as Faith

Brook explains: 'If we were on the air live we couldn't afford to blow the lines and as sets were more often than not closed, there was no obvious place for a prompter, so we usually made up a lot of rubbish and somehow muddled through. I remember an older actor in his first TV appearance worried that he might forget his lines, asking how he got a prompt. He was told to go to the nearest opening in the set – a door or window – and to pull his right earlobe. Unfortunately the actor in question had a habit of doing this in real life, and consequently the play went out as a series of prompts and very little dialogue!'

Peter Byrne describes how certain mannerisms operated as a kind of code. 'Rubbing your nose meant "Look out, I don't think I know the next line." Pulling your ear meant "Oh God, I think I've gone." It was a signal to your opposite number, but it was unconscious. Jack [Warner] used to sniff and I'd think, "Whoops, here we go!"' Byrne remembers Jack Warner, the eponymous hero of *Dixon of Dock Green*, suffering badly on one occasion. 'Jack was terrified of [drying] and we had this dreadful incident which was legendary in the BBC, where I made up a three-act play about something I couldn't possibly know. Jack was getting on a bit and he had the lead lines every week. I had this agreement with the PA that he would never, ever use the dreaded cut key, because if Jack dried I would get him out of it and vice versa. Jack trusted me and because he had started in variety he would rise to the occasion – if I ad-libbed he would ad-lib back. On this classic occasion it was the one episode where the whole thing was geared to circumstantial evidence that I couldn't possibly know, but that he had found out. I always had a problem with legalese, particularly the way cops speak when they are giving evidence, and I had a load of it and I was somewhat distracted anyway. I wasn't aware that he was struggling. He had an old character actress with him who was also drying and it was a bit of a shambles. Our usual PA was on leave and we had a young girl who panicked and was pushing the cut key down when they were speaking and lifting it up for when she was giving the cue. This happened a couple of times. I was suddenly aware that he was all over the shop. He was standing at the corner of the desk, with two very distinguished actors sitting in front of him, wide-eyed. He started to go and I thought, *Oh Christ, what do I do?* I moved away to get the camera off him and did "I know what you're thinking" kind of acting, summarized the whole thing in thirty seconds in time for them to get on the bit of film that came at the end. It was very apparent what had happened: the telephones started ringing. They smuggled Jack off and sent him home. He did have the flu or a cold and that was the excuse they made. The following week I had all of the lead lines, and all the big boys wanted to record it, and I said, "If you do that you'll destroy him. I've got all the lead lines, I'll get us out of it, trust me. You've got to let him get back on the bicycle." So they did. He had a brief dry during the first minute, but we got out of it and after that he was fine.' The strain of giving a live performance of a lead role must have been colossal to somebody in his late seventies and it is unsurprising that other performers recall Jack Warner sometimes having difficulty with his lines. Harry Landis describes how 'Jack was on the phone and they recorded the other person speaking and Jack got himself one line ahead so he'd say, "Where'd they go?" and the answer would be, "Half-past one." "What time did they get there?" "Victoria Station." Poor old thing was fumbling through and he couldn't quite work out what was going wrong.'

Like Peter Byrne, Faith Brook was skilled at helping out when others dried. 'In New York I worked with many film actors, some very well known indeed. Most of them were very wary of this new medium – I'm sure several of them thought it would spell the end of their careers – and in consequence they were nervous and shaky on lines. I became known as Old Faithful, as I managed time and again to get them out of trouble and back on course. I may say that this was not conducive to my giving a truthful, concentrated performance!' Among the actors who had the benefit of her assistance was Glyn Houston. 'I did a live television programme with Leslie Phillips and Faith Brook. It was a farce of some kind. I had a long scene with Faith where we ordered drinks and an essential part of the plot was that she got me drunk. We ordered the drinks and by the time they should have turned up nothing had arrived. I could see lines coming up like nails in a coffin. As a young actor I couldn't think what to do. Suddenly, when we got to the point when we should have been saying, "Cheers!" Faith said, "Where the hell is that waiter with the drinks?" And she shouted, "Waiter!" And behind the door we heard this rattle of bottles and glasses. Our fellow-actor had completely gone to sleep and the poor thing brought the glasses on absolutely shaking.'

In the absence of stalwart colleagues who could be relied upon to come to the rescue, some actors took to writing crib notes for themselves, with varying degrees of success. George Baker relates that 'In *The Square Ring* one of the cast could not learn his lines, or he pretended he could not learn his lines and he wrote cribs on gaffer tape and he put them on the floor. We all knew our lines, but there was a little pause while this chap looked down and then said his. When we came to the actual transmission he had picked up all his bits of white tape and was absolutely fluent and word-perfect and we were all twitching away because we didn't expect it. We'd grown so used to having a little pause while he looked for his line.' Stephen Hancock remembers a similar occurrence in *Emergency Ward 10*. 'Charles Tingwell played one of the surgeons. He used to cut his script up into lines and stick them together with Sellotape until it formed one long strip. He used to pull it along the operating table, reading from it as he went.' Another solution recalled by Hancock proved more fallible than the Sellotape method: 'One of the doctors had to do a consultation with a patient, at the end of which he had to go to the basin saying, "Well, Mrs So-and-so, you've got hydropharconphlyconitis!" It was the technical, medical jargon that none of us could cope with. And he could never remember this word. He got a marker pen and wrote it on the basin and it went fine at the dress rehearsal. Come the performance, he turned the tap on and there was real water coming out and it washed the word away, so he turned to the woman and said, "Well, Mrs Thing, you've got a very rare disease."' Just how unreliable the system of writing lines down could be is demonstrated by another recollection from Harry Landis's days on *Dixon of Dock Green*. 'The man who played the elderly desk sergeant in *Dixon* couldn't remember a line and he had all the pages of his script laid out along the desk and he'd gradually move along from one page to the next. One day some rotten sod mixed up all the pages just before the off.'

According to Peggy Mount, even if your fellow-actors remembered their words, there was no guarantee that they would come out in the right order. 'In one episode [of *The Larkins*] we had an actress who never ever said a line straight. If you said, "I'm going down the road," she'd say, "Oh was you?" This is live television! The last line of our little scene was, "Old Mrs Johnson did so enjoy her dollops of hyacinth tea." And she said, "Old Mrs Dollop did so enjoy her Johnsons of hyacinth tea"!'

To fail in such a public forum can be a devastating experience for an actor. 'A terrifying thing happened to a friend of mine who was in a live play,' says Josephine Tewson. 'There was one poor actor who hadn't done it before. All the sets were side by side so that the cameras could move from set to set. It was a scene between a very elderly actor and somebody else, and the poor elderly actor got terrible nerves and kept on forgetting his lines. The cut key was going all the time and it was absolutely ghastly. This friend of mine was standing behind the cameras thinking, *Oh that poor man, oh my God, but at least it's going out now and he'll never have to see it.* Anyway, that scene finished and the cameras moved to the next scene, which started, and all of a sudden in between the cameras, in front of one of them, this elderly actor walked across with his head in his hands. There was a sort of unspoken conspiracy that nobody told him.' In such situations the sense of disgrace is exacerbated by the realization you have not just let yourself down, but in doing so have created complications for everyone else involved in the production. Janet Hargreaves points out that 'If you started to ad-lib, the camera cues would go to pot and you would hear this terrible hissing coming from the gallery through the cans of the PA. You'd pick up the tension.'

4

ITV: The New Kid on the Block 1955–64

ONE OF THE most significant events in the history of broadcasting was the inauguration in 1955 of commercial television. The Conservative government of the day believed that the BBC's monopoly fostered inefficiency and denied the public any choice. A number of vested interests, including the manufacturers of television sets, advertisers and some performers and writers, were quick to adopt this point of view. Ranged against them were people involved in the Church and education, who suspected that television was a malign influence anyway, and a number of newspaper proprietors who feared that such a venture would poach advertising revenue from their own businesses. According to Dallas Bower, those working for the BBC itself were understandably horrified by the prospect: 'For most of us who had pioneered the foundation of a regular television service under the auspices of the BBC, the introduction of commercial television American-style into the United Kingdom seemed a total violation of all that is meant by the words "public service broadcasting".'

Battle-lines were drawn over the issue of quality. Supporters of the status quo feared that independent television would cater for populist taste and appeal to the lowest common denominator – anathema to the aspirational ethos of the BBC – whilst those in favour of breaking the monopoly insisted that competition would drive quality *up*. The matter was put to a vote in Parliament and in 1954 the Television Bill was passed, paving the way for the launch of ITV. On 22 September 1955 the newly established network televised a ceremony at the Guildhall in London marking the start of its own service. The BBC did its utmost to sabotage the occasion by choosing this night to kill off Grace Archer, one of the best-loved characters in the long-running radio soap. Even so, 188,000 households in possession of the necessary receivers were able to watch the launch of commercial television.

Unlike the original vision for BBC TV, which was from the outset based primarily in London, ITV was conceived in terms of a number of regional centres contributing to a central network. The screenwriter Dick Sharples recalls how the system worked: 'ITV didn't have a central scheduler as they do now; they had a network committee where Lew Grade and all the others would sit round the table and say, "If you take mine, I'll take yours." It was horse-trading.' Adrian Cairns provides an example: 'One day in the presentation office the phone rang and I picked it up. "Granada here, Stuart Burge speaking. We're thinking of putting out a new show, but it's a Lancashire thing. We don't know if you'd like to take it in Newcastle because it's a bit Lancashire-orientated. We're going to do thirteen episodes. Tentative title – *Coronation Street*." '

The companies involved in this process were Associated Rediffusion, who had the franchise for London during the week; Associated Television, who had bid for London at the weekend and the Midlands during the week; ABC Television, who broadcast to the Midlands and the North at the weekend; and Granada, who provided a service to the North during the week. These fledgeling companies were starting from scratch and had to provide themselves with both studios and staff. Dick Sharples explains how they set about the former. 'In the fifties, Rediffusion and ATV were buying up all the old theatres and converting them into instant television studios – the Hackney Empire, the Wood Green Empire and the Chiswick Empire.' Keith Martin recalls the conditions of work further north: 'The ABC studios in Didsbury were a converted cinema and David Hamilton and I, who worked in the Presentation Department, used to sit in what we called the broom cupboard. At the time ABC had the franchise for the whole of the North of England, covering what would now be Yorkshire Television, Granada Television and Central [i.e. Carlton Central].'

The matter of staff was equally pressing, according to David London, who worked for commercial television in its earliest days. 'The new ITV companies were looking for people who had worked in television. A lot of the new staff were ex-BBC who could see the new possibilities – a number of them went from assistant cameraman to senior cameraman overnight, just like that, because they were desperate for people.' Not only did ITV poach staff from the BBC but also the presenter David Hamilton recalls that in his early days as a continuity announcer, ABC tried to emulate the formal ethos of the Corporation, certainly with regards to the matter of dress. 'In October 1960 I went up as an announcer for ABC. In those days you appeared in vision [on screen]. There was just a camera and a clock in front of you, and some very intricate timing to do. I felt very raw. In the evening after seven o'clock we wore dinner jackets and bow ties. It was a hangover from the Reithian days at the BBC . . . I had to borrow a dinner jacket and bow tie from John Benson, who was a lot taller and a lot slimmer than me. The jacket wouldn't do up, leaving a vast expanse of white, and the sleeves were too long so I had to keep my hands under the desk. Eventually they bought me a dinner suit, although very often you didn't bother with the trousers as you were only seen from the waist up. We would often wear shorts under the desk in the summer.' Casting practices at some of the ITV companies could be as idiosyncratic as at the BBC, George Baker recalls: 'In November 1957 I did *Death of a Salesman* and it was adapted by Stanley Mann, so you got stunning stuff . . . I'd worked with the director before and he wanted me to play Biff, but [Sidney] Bernstein [founder of Granada Television] said, "George Baker is a film actor, he can't do television, not a role like that." Eventually the director rang me up and said, "Now look, this is a terrible thing to do to an actor. If you want to play it Sidney says that he will let you rehearse for two weeks on probation, so what do you want to do?" Well, of course, who would turn down the opportunity of playing Biff? In those days there was quite often a probationary period of rehearsal, but it's very cruel. The director was wonderful, absolutely wonderful, very supportive. We did the rehearsal period, and then they came – Sidney Bernstein, Stanley Mann – and we did the rehearsal for them. We did about three scenes and we were sent away to the pub. And there we sat waiting for the great decision, absolutely wrung out. Then the director came in, brightly smiling. I think we cancelled rehearsals for the rest of the day and got drunk. It was the most successful television that Granada had ever had. It got the most incredible notices.'

Baker also had the embarrassment of being offered a part by being mistaken for somebody else. He joined a fantastic cast that included Alan Bates, Sean Connery and Alfred Burke in *The Square Ring*, which was a *Play of the Week* in June 1959. 'As I walked into the rehearsal room I looked at the face of the director and said, "You wanted Stanley, didn't you?" He said, "No. No. No." I said, "Well, I'll go if you like," and he said, "No." But he did want Stanley Baker.' (Such confusion is not unique. Miriam Karlin recalls, 'I was in Bing [Crosby]'s Christmas show and I had just been on holiday to Israel. I tan very easily, I really was very seriously brown and in those days my hair was dark. Shirley Bassey was in the show. At the read-through the only people who were there were those who were doing sketches with Bing. Shirley wasn't there. Bing's manager was sitting on the sofa with Rose Tobias Shaw, who was the casting director. He was looking across at me and then he turned to her and said, "Shirley Bassey looks a little Jewish, doesn't she?" ')

In order to guarantee the quality of commercial television's output, the Independent Television Authority was established to regulate the new channel and to ensure the network informed, educated and entertained its audience. However, within two years of opening ITV was transmitting as many as ten quiz shows a week. The most famous of these both originated on Radio Luxembourg but were successfully transferred to television in 1955 and ran concurrently until 1968. David London was involved with both: 'I worked on *Take Your Pick* and *Double Your Money*. I did *Take Your Pick* mostly because I got on well with Michael Miles [the presenter]. The difference between those programmes and quiz programmes now is that they genuinely picked the people out of the studio audience. They tried to pick people with a bit of spark; in a way it was their personalities that were important, not whether they could answer the questions.' Because quizzes such as these offered cash prizes of up £1,000, a huge amount of money at that time, the public was spellbound and ITV started to surge ahead in the ratings. This was a concern to many who had expressed misgivings about the maintenance of quality programming, and in order to address their doubts and to examine the effects of the launch of its rival on the BBC, in 1960 the government set up a public inquiry into the state of television as a whole, under the auspices of Sir Harry Pilkington.

Commercial television received no funding whatsoever from the state, deriving all its revenue from advertising. Andrew Crisell describes the conditions attached to such an arrangement:

> The 1954 Television Act carefully defined those products and services which could not be advertised, and though many prohibitions have remained constant, some have been lifted and fresh ones imposed. The act forbade advertising with a political or

religious aim, or on any public question on which there could be more than one opinion, such as abortion or capital punishment. No commercials could be broadcast for money-lenders, matrimonial agencies or fortune tellers. On the grounds that they might offend public taste there could be no adverts for condoms or, until the late 1970s, for female sanitary products. Cigarette commercials were not banned until August 1965, yet before 1971 no female could be seen modelling underwear except in silhouette.

The acting profession viewed the prospect of working in commercials with ambivalence. Peggy Mount raised an objection shared by many: 'I've been offered the earth to do adverts and I never would do them because I knew that I wouldn't be Peggy Mount any more, I'd be the advert. For a couple of years you earned a lot of money, but the income tax took it all anyway.' Wendy Craig suggests that the resistance was initially quite widespread. 'Doing television commercials was definitely not on. When we saw the money that they were paying, everybody quickly changed their minds.' The fees were indeed persuasive and before long many actors were only too willing to take on this kind of work, even committing themselves for a considerable length of time. Hilary Mason says, 'I was the Hotpoint lady for a whole year. I advertised washing machines, electric fires, fridges. There was a clause in my contract that said I wasn't allowed to advertise anything else or take on any work that would interfere with the two days in the middle of the month when they wanted me.'

The various regional companies were autonomous and sold their own advertising space, and Adrian Cairns reveals that this could sometimes lead to confusion: 'The

ABC in those days ran two stations, Yorkshire and Lancashire, from two transmitters, and they put out different [live] commercial breaks for the same programmes. You'd be doing an *Armchair Theatre* from Didsbury and you would have one commercial break for Manchester and Liverpool, and another for Leeds. You had to stay in control and not get them muddled up. I remember on one occasion a commercial for Camay soap went out with a soundtrack for beef sausages.' Even if the schedulers beamed the right commercial to the right region, there were considerable stresses for the actors on the studio floor. 'I was hired to do a commercial live in London for the *People*. Their crime reporter was Duncan Webb and I had to interview him about a bloodstained piece of wood that was discovered in a murder investigation. I had sixty seconds live at peak time on a Saturday evening, and just before I was due to go on, the Managing Director came up to me and said, "Well, Mr Cairns, you'll get it right, won't you? I've got £500,000 on you for this one!" I said, "Thank you very much. Why didn't you tell me afterwards and not before?"' He goes on to describe some of the challenges involved: 'Have you ever tried to demonstrate a collapsing table for ironing, live on television? You were up against the advertisers, who always wanted something impossible – changing lines at the last minute, without realizing that would alter the whole rhythm of what you were doing.' Maurice Denham also remembers a certain amount of intervention from the companies whose products were being promoted. 'In the early days I did a lot of voiceovers for Cadbury's Roses and at one point I got a letter from Cadbury's saying, "Our output is chocolate, not choclit!"'

The stakes were certainly high and Roger Ostime recalls that if a mistake was made, such as misquoting the product's price, the television company had to forgo its fee.

According to Stephen Hancock, for those not involved in the sixty seconds of intense stress of an advert, the commercial break could be welcome. 'When you were working for ITV the commercial breaks came as a wonderful relief. You would do your two or three scenes and then this wonderful floor manager would say, "On commercials!", and you knew that you had two or three minutes to sort yourself out, although usually you were either changing or getting yourself to another part of the studio. It did mean you had a breather. For the technicians it was much harder. They had to do everything in those couple of minutes; they had to reset the scene, change the props, do all sorts of things, and all the cameras and sound crews had to relocate.' This latter point is endorsed by stage manager Margaret Tabor: 'Working for ITV was much harder discipline because you had to be on time for the commercial breaks. In a half-hour production the play would last about twenty-seven minutes, the first commercial break would come at about twelve minutes fifty-seven seconds and it would last about two minutes twenty-seven seconds. By comparison people at the BBC had it easy because they were working to the minute and to the foot of film, while ITV were running to the second and to the inch of film.' David London explains the harsh reality: 'Programmes had to finish on time and they had to stop for the commercial breaks on time. If you hadn't finished the programme, they ran the commercials anyway because they couldn't afford not to. If they didn't run them, they didn't get the money.'

Presenters often suffered at the hands of poor time keepers, and David Hamilton remembers how 'One Sunday night the show at the London Palladium which we were broadcasting live underran by three minutes, which left me three minutes to talk to camera. I picked up the *TV Times* and talked about the rest of the programmes for that night, then I talked about all the programmes for Monday and some of the programmes for Tuesday as well! You were like the goalkeeper in a football team, you were the last line of defence.'

There were however occasions when the iron grip of the commercial break was relaxed. For the first play that ITV ever did about the Holocaust, *The Investigation* by Peter Weiss, it was considered unsuitable to transmit advertisements during the performance. For Eve Pearce, 'It was one of the most remarkable experiences that I have ever had in my whole life. There were only two women in it and something like thirty men. The format of the play was the trial; there were six witnesses, four men and two women and they represented all the people who went through the camps. We worked in huge rehearsal rooms with pillars and all over the room the director had pasted documentary evidence – you couldn't look anywhere without seeing it or reading it. The script was based on verbatim accounts. That meant you couldn't act it, you had to go as close to the experience as you could. I think I'm right in saying that it was the only time that ITV did not run adverts.'

When ITV first went on air, as well as running adverts during shows it also devised themed mini-programmes that consisted entirely of commercials. These were known as 'advertising magazines', 'ad mags' for short. David

London worked as a technician on *Jim's Inn*, 'The idea was that Jimmy Handley would be behind the bar talking to various customers: "Have you tried this new beer?" "Ooh, that's very tasty. Eh, what are you smoking over there?" There were little bits of narrative in between, they'd have a little bit of chat about the pigs or the lady down the road, then they'd say, "Have you tried this new brand of pig feed?"' He goes on to explain that featuring the product prominently was vital. 'The pack shot was the most important thing. They'd spend hours lining these pack shots up. You rehearsed it and the position of the pack would be marked so that when it went out live the actor could put it down in exactly the right place. The advertisers would be saying, "No, I can't have it on the table, I want it on the bar."'

Leslie Lawton recalls another of the most famous ad mags. 'In *What's in Store* with Doris Rogers, she was meant to be the manageress of a department store and she'd go round saying, "Oh that's interesting, what are you selling there? That's new in, is it?"' Paul Williamson did a stint in Doris Rogers's so-called department store: 'We all had to demonstrate various things and mine was a make of carpet. I had five different carpets, eight different shades and several different prices to remember. It was terrible, having to demonstrate the depth and quality of the pile in close-up, but a new carpet actually comes away, so I was having to palm the fluff while I was showing the carpet off: "It comes in bronze and old-fashioned black . . . !" I think that was the lowest I've ever come. In the same programme there was a girl having to demonstrate a magnificent refrigerator. To show how much it held she unloaded the whole thing and put the stuff on the table, then she had endless trouble getting it all back in, she only just managed it and that was live! The man from the advertising agency and one representing the product would be in the studio with you and they would keep rushing up and giving you notes, and they might be quite different from what the director was saying.'

Roger Ostime recalls another format that was more successful. 'There was one done by John Warren and John Singer which really was a story. It was set in a block of flats and they were the janitors. They would meet various residents and pass them on so-called tips – "Don't forget your Davenport's beer-at-home service!" These little programmes lasted about twenty minutes and were broadcast once a fortnight or once a week.'

A brief commercial could be as technically complicated as a full-blown play. 'I did a travel ad mag called *Where Shall We Go?*,' says Leslie Lawton. 'There were lots of sketches – a sketch of a funny thing happening in Spain, and then you'd get the details of how to travel there. This entailed lots of costume changes. These would quite often happen while you were in close-up; you'd have to try and keep still while someone was sticking your foot down a trouser-leg.'

Venetia Barrett worked on an ad mag called *A New Kind of Party* and has kept a copy of her script. On the front it states, 'This recording session involves Venetia Barrett and Jack Parnell and his orchestra.' The fact that a whole orchestra was employed gives an idea of the scale of these productions. She recalls that 'The products featured were Superma, which was a home perm, *Woman* magazine, Maxwell House Coffee and Birds Lemon Pie Filling. It started with a dance routine and was quite a long programme in which a number of the actors and actresses did scenes incorporating various products. We all thought it was naff at the time. The presenter Sylvia Peters was very well known as a sort of continuity person. I remember I thought the other girls were absolutely ghastly, I thought I was vastly superior to them because they were the sort of girls who only did commercials and I was a serious actress! There was that distinction in those days, and we all looked down on them terribly. It was rather like the difference between straight performers and variety in acting. Here's a quotation from the script. "Let's all join the party, but a new kind. You may remember that Elsa Maxwell once said, 'The best parties are given by people who can't afford them.' Well we've come here today to tell you about and show you how to organize a party you could have at 11 o'clock in the morning or 11 o'clock at night. . . . You'll get beautifully fresh coffee out of this jar. It's as easy as ABC to make and you'll get real coffee-pot freshness and taste . . . Good hostesses find that lemon meringue pie is perfect for coffee parties. . . . You know *Woman* knitting designs are always so smart and use the newest types of wool. I must do this sweater!"'

The ad mags were banned in 1962 because they blurred the line between advertising and true drama. According to Paul Williamson, 'Now that's been taken over by product placement, which is much more subtle and underhand.' Indeed, in 1962 when Sir Harry Pilkington delivered his report on television, ad mags were prohibited on the grounds that not only was there the potential for confusion between programmes and commercials, but also because they exceeded the amount of time permitted for advertisements in any given hour.

Commercial television as a whole was regarded with a certain amount of prejudice to begin with, by both actors and the general public. According to Michael Kilgarriff, 'There were lots of people who wouldn't watch ITV. It was considered common because of all the commercials. If you were working for them, ITV paid you much better and looked after you much better – cars to take you to and from the studio, free lunches – but there was a tremendous cachet working for the BBC, it was still a magic name. Things were done properly [at the BBC]. Anything that was needed for a show – costumes, sets – was provided.' Janet Hargreaves is broadly in agreement. 'In my experience the BBC spent much more money on their programmes, whereas ATV counted every penny.' Margaret Tyzack believes that 'There was a feeling of professionalism and doing things well that came from the BBC, they set the standards for everything. There were high standards at ITV as well, of course, but they did things that were a little more frivolous.'

Harry Landis confesses, 'As actors we found it very difficult to get on with the commercial breaks. You felt that ITV was somehow cheaper, you felt that if it was quality it would go straight through. The BBC didn't have to worry so much, but ITV had to worry even if the programme was thirty seconds over, because companies bought advertising time down to the last second. You felt that everything was commercial, it was about making money, and we were a sort of fill-in between the commercials. Keep the budgets low for the actors, squeeze as much money as you can from the advertisers and you have a good profit motive there. We always thought quality was on the side of the BBC.'

For Wendy Craig, working for the BBC provided a greater feeling of reassurance. 'When you were working for ITV, there was a great deal of pressure to get the timing right for the commercial breaks. Working for the BBC was much more relaxing, you didn't have to cut so much in rehearsal to allow for the commercials, you had about ten minutes extra. One also felt that they were much more competent, they had been doing it for longer and were much more experienced. You felt you were in slightly safer hands.' Maurice Denham puts it succinctly: 'I don't think there was any difference between ITV and the BBC . . . Ah, that's it, they paid better! I knew there was something in the back of my mind.'

On the subject of pay, Richard Bebb says, 'One of the most disgraceful things the BBC ever did was when ITV was being formed. They were so terrified of this commercial television set-up, that it was going to create competition for actors when the BBC was used to being the only employer, that they actually made an offer to disclose all the fees [paid to actors], which ITV accepted, in an effort to keep them down. From that day to this ITV has always paid better money than the BBC.' Peter Bowles remembers the wariness that characterized the Corporation's attitude to the newcomer. 'There was no difference between the BBC and ITV in terms of talent. Some ITV companies put actors under contract for several years. I have a feeling that if you appeared on ITV you wouldn't be asked to appear on the BBC. I don't think it was the same vice versa. ITV was offering more money to the writers, directors and actors and the BBC were a bit scared of that.'

Several actors are eager to speak up for ITV. James Grout points out that 'The ITV companies had smaller set-ups, they were more self-contained. The BBC was doing lots and lots of different forms of television and they had all these different departments and you felt slightly isolated from the hub and hum of the place. ITV was much smaller – you could open your door and shout and the Head of Drama would come running up the corridor, he was only up the road. You could communicate quicker and more easily. At the BBC you had to go through particular channels and it could take two days to get a message through. Granada and Yorkshire were big and important companies, but they only had one flag flying. The BBC had lots of flags flying – sound-radio as well.' Josephine Tewson echoes his comments: 'The BBC was a much bigger organization than any of the others. There were a lot of people; it was more intimidating in a way because the building was bigger. I used to get lost finding my way to the studio.'

Barbara Lott declares, 'I think ITV in the early days was marvellous. Granada was marvellous – the *Armchair Theatre*. I think that made the BBC really sit up.' Other actors single Granada out for special praise. 'I liked Granada best. They had a very high standard, they took a lot of trouble,' says Edward Jewesbury. Eve Pearce believes the company had a particular strength where drama was concerned: 'The first drama that Granada ever did was six half-hour plays and they only went out in the region. They had to be done at eleven o'clock at night because Sidney [Bernstein] thought that nobody would watch them . . . One of them was written by a man who was a floor manager at Granada in those days, his name was John Hopkins. He went on to become editor of *Z Cars* when that came to be born. Anyway, he produced the script and it was called *Break Up*. Granada was wonderful because it would look at new plays.' Granada's reputation for television drama extended well beyond the period covered by this book, culminating in such landmark productions as *Brideshead Revisited* (1981) and *The Jewel in the Crown* (1984).

Indeed, since one of the recommendations of Pilkington's report was that the BBC should be licensed to establish a new channel, one could argue that the advent of independent television ultimately paved the way for the foundation of the more intellectually rigorous BBC2; and in this and through its own input, it did significantly enlarge the choice available to viewers in Britain.

ITV's promotion of new drama specifically written for television in its *Armchair Theatre* series (1956–9) provoked the Corporation into a review of its own policies with regard to the transmission of plays, which led to a flowering of television drama in the shape of *The Wednesday Play* (1964–70), *Play for Today* (1970–84), *Play of the Month* (1965–79) and *Play of the Week* (1977–9).

Faith Brook points out that, when she started work in television in 1949, 'They were all live shows then, stage plays adapted for TV, usually sixty to ninety minutes long.' In other words, producers and directors were still clinging to the theatrical tradition with which they were familiar, but by the mid-1950s the wind of change was blowing and writers were being commissioned to produce work tailored to television's particular requirements. 'The things they did . . . tended to be contemporary drama, not classical plays,' says Peter Bowles. 'This meant that the manner of speech and the emotions were absolutely of today. They were written for television, written to be filmed in front of a camera.'

5

In Studio

To UNDERSTAND THE trials faced by actors working in live television, it is helpful to have an idea of the geography of a studio. Michael Kilgarriff offers a description: 'The sets were built round the edge of the studio in a circle, leaving a space in the middle for the cameras. You would be standing in one set with your hand on a door knob waiting for the previous scene to finish and a camera would come gliding across the floor to you like a Dalek, followed by another, and you knew the scene was getting closer, then the studio manager would come rushing over and give you a cue.' Because of the size of the early Emitron cameras, manoeuvring was problematic, and director Leonard Lewis describes the solution: 'The way the sets were placed in the studio was very important. It was no use having a set next to another set when you were cutting from one to the other because it would be very difficult for the cameras to regroup. You always cut from one scene to another as far away as possible. There was quite an art in the way the designer and the director worked it out. The designer would come to your office with his plan on transparent paper and using Sellotape you would move sets around.'

Poor benighted performers were often faced with a sprint the length of the studio in order to get from one scene to the next. Alec McCowen gives an evocation of what this could be like: 'There were several sets built all round the studio and as soon as you came off one there would be a person waiting to lead you to the other, because you never had any idea where you had to go next, and there were all these wires and things all over the place and they had to stop you tripping over. Sometimes you'd only have a minute to get from one set to another and you'd have to do a quick change as well.' Often extra dialogue had to be written to facilitate this, according to John Warner: 'In order to be changed ready for the next scene, quite often you would be saying your lines while going round behind the camera and taking your trousers off. A lot of extra scenes had to be written to give the actor time for these changes, which must have made the plays seem rather pedantic.'

Josephine Tewson remembers that the need for speedy costume changes often put the performer in a tight spot. 'Because it was live you had the most horrific costume changes because you had to be out of one thing and into something else in no time at all. The first one I did was in a children's television programme. I was doing a monologue as Sarah Siddons or someone, talking about in her youth having to walk to Bristol to be an actress. I had a quick change into something else straight afterwards, with the result that during the last half-page of dialogue, which I was delivering to camera, the wardrobe ladies were busy taking off my skirt and my petticoat and the boots that I was in. How I remembered my lines while this was being done, trying not to be pulled about and not to wobble, I don't know to this day. It's a sort of recurring nightmare whenever I think about it.'

Paul Williamson says that sometimes there was simply not enough time to achieve a smooth transition from one scene to the next. 'Often a duologue would start with the camera on one person while the other raced to get into position, and you could see the panic in the eyes of the actor until his colleague arrived.' The sense of speed occasionally spilled over into the performance itself. Maurice Denham remembers, 'I was in a play where I had to do a lot of entrances into offices and entrances into dining rooms and corridors. When I got home my wife said, "You were so brisk, you kept bursting into scenes!" But you had to be, the camera would be there waiting for you. There might be a man sitting there playing a scene to nobody, while you got your costume changed and got yourself there.' Harry Landis explains that, with the best will in the world, performers could not always arrive at the next scene on time: 'I was in an episode of *The Avengers* and I got a copy of one of the live ones and I watched it recently. Someone went to a door and they cut to the new room where the door was going to open and this person was going to come in, and it took ages. There was a ten-second shot of a door and a wall.'

According to George Cole, 'The commonest problem with live TV was dead bodies getting up and walking away.' If even the dead could not be depended upon, what hope for the hapless live performer? A number made unscheduled appearances – Alec McCowen relates how 'People would wander into shot and block you off without realising what they were doing, and you'd just have to dodge round them and get back into shot.' Some appearances could be particularly hard to explain away, such as this one, recounted by Richard Bebb: 'Gwen Watford did a play set on the eighteenth floor of a building in New York and one of the carpenters accidentally walked past the window.'

Writer Dick Sharples recalls an equally disastrous visitation: 'The first television series we got away [succeeded in making] was called *Steve Hunter, Trouble Merchant*. We knew we couldn't have a lot of sets, so we had one standard set and moved it about the world. They constructed a motor torpedo boat and we had floating detectives who moved all round the world. All we had to do was to put up a film clip of Gibraltar and there they were. One day I went to the Wood Green Empire, where it was being transmitted. They had a few basic sets: the kitchen set, the boat-deck set and a backcloth that had a huge seascape on it. The actors had to move from set to set. I stood watching with a security man and an actor was caught on shot tiptoeing across the seascape. The security man said, "Bloody hell, it's the first time that's been done since Jesus Christ!"'

According to Adrian Cairns, sometimes artists from completely different studios would drop by. 'At Tyne Tees they had a kind of variety show at lunchtime. They had Spike Milligan on one day. The two studios were adjacent and I was reading the local news in Studio One and he had just finished in Studio Two and he came into the news studio, a complete lord of misrule, while I was reporting on a bus accident.' Nigel Hawthorne witnessed somebody making a desperate bid for her moment in the limelight: 'There was one thing I did at the Riverside Studios, Rudolf Cartier was directing it, it was an opera called *The Saint of Bleeker Street*. I do remember on one occasion when we were in transmission in the studio and one of the women, Virginia Copeland, had to get up and sing this long aria. While she was singing the aria, she had to move slowly backwards, find a chair, fall down on the chair, and the stigmata which were on the palms of her hands had then to be revealed. Just before she did that, this girl who was in the chorus with me suddenly decided that she wanted to be seen on television and flung herself into the chair as Virginia Copeland was backing towards it. I and the person sitting next to me raced to the chair and got the girl out of it, hauled her off the set and locked her into the lavatory, so we weren't actually in the scene at all.'

If actors were not coping with colleagues' unscripted appearances, they were often dealing with their unrehearsed absence. John Warner 'did a religious programme involving a couple who were being given advice about marriage from a man who was at that time a religious adviser to Princess Margaret. As part of the action we were to be offered cigarettes to smoke. We rehearsed this and came to transmission and we were called down to the set. I thought I'd better just check our props were there, checked the cigarette box and found that it was empty. I rushed back up to my dressing room to get my own cigarettes and when I came down the studio doors were shut. I don't know how I got on to the set eventually, but it was only a minute before transmission and I wasn't there!'

James Grout remembers an incident with the legendary Wilfred Lawson, famously unpredictable as a result of his drinking. 'Wilfred Lawson was staying at a pub over the road from the Granada studios. He was playing a tramp. We did the dress rehearsal and after that he disappeared, he went out of the front door over the road to the pub, dressed, I may say, as this tramp. He did look very effective. Then they changed the bloke on the door! It was a seven-thirty start and at round about seven Wilfred tried to get back in. They wouldn't let him in. "Oh come on, I'm in this play." "Go on, shove off." He had to go round the back, climb a fence and get in through the car park.'

Harry Towb remembers seeing an actor miss an entrance not once but twice during the same programme. 'A famous BBC producer called Howard Rose was doing a play about the French Revolution and he had the idea of having three conspirators with Irish accents, standing around a lamppost quietly discussing matters. They only had two scenes. One of these actors was selling the Irish sweepstake tickets to the cast. There was no green-room, so he retired to a corner of the studio, and leaning on a grand piano was making out receipts for the tickets he had sold. He missed the first scene, which was terrible because it was live. The play was in two parts with an interval for some music or the news. The actor went up to another of the conspirators, a well-known Irish actor called Harry Hutchinson who had covered up for him, and said, "Oh God, Harry, I don't know what I'm gonna do." Harry said, "Just write Howard little note of apology, it'll be fine." So the second act started with him writing a note of apology and he missed the second scene!'

If such occasions arise, it is as well to have a cast-iron excuse prepared. Barbara Lott pays tribute to a colleague's mastery of this art. 'We did a production of *Trelawny of the Wells* and Fabia Drake was playing Mrs Telfer. She and her husband had a flat in a castle in Wales. We rehearsed for a fortnight, on the Monday we had the tech and on the Tuesday we were due to broadcast. I remember the director Michael Barry, a lovely man, saying, "I want you all here very prompt on Monday. Half-past ten on the dot, we're off! The tech boys are coming and they've got to go on to another technical." We all arrived at about quarter-past ten, had a cup of coffee, we were waiting around and there was no sign of Fabia. Eventually one of the technicians said, "I'm sorry, Michael, but we're going to have to start." We did about three pages, then the door was flung open and Fabia stood there and said, "I'm terribly sorry I'm late, I couldn't get the drawbridge down."'

Once on air, according to Maurice Denham, the penalties for overrunning were punitive. 'They did threaten to take plays off if they overran. Lines or even scenes would be chopped.' The knock-on effects were less drastic if a programme underran, as the television companies had short time-filling films on standby. Judy Campbell describes the fare: 'In between the programmes they used to play the potter's wheel going round and round, or they'd show you seagulls coming in and going *squawk, squawk,* with waves breaking underneath them. The potter's wheel had to go round and round for a long time if you underran. They had stage managers standing there waving their hands to slow you down, or making circular motions to speed you up.' Wendy Craig recalls that sometimes the stage managers would have to waylay actors and pass on messages from the director. 'I remember doing *Skyline For Two*, in which I had millions of changes on the run, and we were running short of time and the floor manager grabbed me and said, "Could you speak a little faster?" '

On occasions the fault was a technical one and beyond the artists' control. These tended to be larger-scale disasters, for which merely cutting an occasional speech was an inadequate solution. David London worked as a stage manager and recalls that 'On one occasion the network went off the air for some reason; there was some sort of electrical failure. We were in the middle of some show and we went off the air and after ten minutes we were told it would be at least five minutes before we went back on. During that time the director came down on the floor and went through the script and said, "All right, we'll lose Scene Three, we'll take this page out of Scene Four . . ." and so on. The actors had been told, but they were desperately trying to remember their lines anyway, so we had to go round reminding them all the time – "This page here has gone, you go straight on to this one now." '

Harry Landis was involved in another disaster: 'I was in a children's series with one episode a week. It was in two halves with a commercial break in the middle. One week we came out of the first half going, "Phew! What set are we in for the second half?" when the director suddenly said, "Listen, everybody, you've got to do the last two pages again." "Why?" "Never mind why, just do it again. Then go straight on into the second half." It emerged that just before those two pages there was a fade and the Anglia Television area of the country thought that was the commercial-break time and they started running the commercials while we were doing the last two pages to the rest of the nation. So they started the rest of the programme two pages early for the people who had missed it and the rest of the country could pick up where they left off at the right time for the second half.'

Occasionally disruptions were due to outside events. John Warner described how the Queen Mother's birthday affected the television schedule: 'In the 1960s Peter Dews did a series of the Shakespeare histories called *The Age of Kings*. On the Queen Mother's sixtieth birthday in 1960 Peter Dews was given instructions by Buckingham Palace that we were not allowed to overrun into the news, which you were occasionally allowed to do in those days, because they were showing a documentary about the Queen Mother. Poor Peter had to come into the studio the day before transmission and say, "I don't want any arguments, these are the cuts, we've got to cut out a quarter of an hour." Frank Windsor was playing the English Soldier and I think he had his entire part cut.'

Brian Murphy relates how an episode of *Z Cars* had to be curtailed in order for the BBC to broadcast the exploits of NASA. 'It was at a time when the American astronauts were going into space and that was all being covered live. First they put us back and then they sent a note requesting that we lop some minutes off so that they could catch up with themselves by the end of the evening. The director John McGrath had to work out which five minutes, where. All the cameras had been plotted and blocked and so had the actors. There wasn't much time to work it out. They found there was one scene that they could chop because it had nothing to do with the plot, it was literally a filler in order for the principal actor in the following scene to change his costume. He had to go from his full costume as a policeman into his pyjamas and sit placidly at the breakfast table talking to his wife. He put his pyjamas on under his uniform and he had to hurtle from one end of the studio to the other. He tore everything off and they kept the camera rolling on his wife preparing the cornflakes and talking as if her husband were sitting at the chair. He arrived so out of breath he couldn't get a word out. He filled his mouth with cornflakes and on the second pant they all blew out.'

As if there were not already enough hazards to deal with, the performers who were struggling to keep their heads above water in the days of live television were sometimes confounded by inanimate objects. These could vary in shape and size from a sherry glass to an entire wall. Constance Chapman fell victim to the former. 'I was in a play with Jill Bennett and I was a little Welsh maid and in one scene I had to hand round sherry glasses to everybody. In rehearsal the designer noticed that the tray the glasses were on was very shabby and he asked for it to be varnished. I came on and nobody could get any of the glasses off the tray because they'd stuck to the varnish. I had to go round saying, "You don't want any sherry, do you?", shaking my head. You felt so terrible when things went wrong, your heart stopped.' Miss Chapman's heart stopped on more than one occasion: 'I remember playing Maureen Pryor's sister and she in the play was a compulsive smoker and we had a long scene about smoking and Stage Management had forgotten to set the cigarettes.

Maureen had to go off and get a pack. I was left alone and so I plumped up the cushions, I hummed not very success-fully – was I glad to see her return!' For Chapman, bad things came in threes. 'I had to empty a large bowl of water down the sink, making great play with the water, while saying to my mother, "Drowning is a pleasant death, so they do say." But the stage management hadn't put any-thing under the sink to catch the water, so it went all over me and everywhere I walked after that there were pools of water.'

Even if the props were in place, they could not be guar-anteed to work, as Edward Jewesbury discovered to his cost. 'When the BBC moved to Lime Grove there was a children's programme called *Gary Halliday*. I played a police inspector. I was on the phone in one part of the studio, talking to my boss in Scotland Yard, and he was on the phone on the other side of the studio. Suddenly the phone went dead. I couldn't hear him and he couldn't hear me. In the end we put the phones down and shouted across the studio at each other – and that was live!' Another 'tele-phone moment' is recounted by Peter Byrne: 'I had to answer the telephone, but they didn't need the whole set so they just put the telephone on a flat, which was braced. I was standing there having this telephone conversation which was quite long, and in the middle of it I suddenly realized that they hadn't braced it properly and the thing was starting to topple. I put my arm up against it and hero-ically went on, as one did, and at the end of the scene the lights went up and they all left me. In the end I just thought, *Sod it*, and left it and the whole thing went *crash*.'

Hilary Mason did 'a children's programme with a man

called Humphrey Lastocq playing the lead. He was playing a very nice man, but somebody was trying to kill him. One of the ways in which they were trying to kill him was to drop a chandelier down on his head. This chandelier was suspended from a cable and two men were gradually going to let it down. We were all chatting away and the chandelier could not be made to move. Humphrey started making up some dialogue and still nothing happened so in the end he had to shoot himself accidentally.'

Many types of props went astray; according to John Warner the furniture could not always be depended upon to be in place. 'There was a lovely story of Jill Bennett, I think it was, doing a play set in a kitchen and somebody hadn't set a kitchen chair, and she had to play the whole scene perched with her legs crossed, looking as though she was sitting in a chair.' Faced with the same situation, the actor Donald Hewlett did at least receive some help: 'A chair wasn't set where I was supposed to sit and the PA lay on the floor with a crooked elbow and I did the scene sitting on the palm of her hand.'

During the transmission of an episode from a series called *The Pattern of Marriage* by Ted Willis, Peter Byrne found himself with a worse difficulty. 'Billie Whitelaw and I were in a scene . . . I was supposed to be studying, having come out of the Army with no qualifications. We were living in one room in Mum's house, with all the pressures on us, we had a baby which was behind a screen. There were two rather delightful scenes. In one I was sitting at my desk and Billie had been alone all day; she was knitting and the baby was asleep behind the screen. She wanted to talk because she'd been alone and I was trying to study and we had a big row and then the baby cried. We gravitated behind the screen, looked at the baby, looked at one another and she said, "I'll make you a cup of cocoa." The only thing was, they were two almost identical scenes and we went behind the screen and as we came back we found that the stage hands were removing all the furniture. We looked at one another and then we kept going, you just did in live television. They left us one piece of furniture, which was an armchair, so we stuck very close to one another. One of the stage hands hissed at us, "Oh sorry" – they thought we were doing the second scene! Then suddenly they realized and all hell was let loose. The light went out on the top of the camera, the lights came up on a café set at the other end of the studio where all the actors were sitting waiting, and they leaped into action.' This production seems to have been fraught with problems: 'Before the marriage when we were in our separate houses, they kept cutting between us. I was restless in bed and so was she. I was lying in the bed and looking at the clock and so was she. To save space they just had a narrow flat with the bed clothes pinned to it and they stood you up against it and shot it as though it were taken from overhead. But they tied us in! Off they shot and I couldn't move, I was like Houdini struggling: "Help! Help!"'

And there were times when help was seriously, urgently required. Incidents involving physical harm to performers range from the trivial to the fatal. Eve Pearce recalls a minor injury: 'In the early days of Granada, Sidney Bernstein was very keen on the region itself, so he did a series of documentaries about things that went on in [Manchester] at night. In one of these they got hold of a top gynaecologist to do a Caesarean section. They didn't want a live Caesarean section, they didn't pretend that it was real, but they did want to show it as well as possible. What they did was to intercut with a piece of film showing the actual baby coming out, but for all of the previous bit they had me. There was I, lying on the bed, covered with this green cloth with just a hole cut out of it. They had to clip it to make sure it didn't slip during the operation and the clip went into my skin. It was agony, I was reduced to whispering desperately, "Clip! Clip!" There was a nurse standing next to me and she didn't even realize it was me for a long time, because I was so anxious not to be heard by the microphone. I couldn't wait until the end of the transmission, it was so painful, it was awful.'

For an actor to receive the odd knock or bump seems to have been par for the course and Nigel Hawthorne was no exception. 'It was in those days quite amateurish. In *Hurrah for Halloween*, which was an eighteenth-century sort of thing, a bit like *Cinderella*, I remember I had to come on and present Joan Sims with her broomstick. I was wearing the full flunkey's outfit. Somebody missed an entrance and I was told to move like lightning all the way round the back of the set and come through the doors. As I did so I remember tripping over a brace and falling absolutely headlong, knocking my wig over my eye.'

Hawthorne also recalled witnessing another performer hit the deck. 'Doing a live performance you just had to trust that the technical things would go well . . . I did a live programme for Associated Rediffusion, who had some studios in Kingsway. I remember one of the cameras backing into an actor who was standing watching a

Douglas Birkinshaw with the Marconi EMI instantaneous television camera transmitting pictures of the view from Alexandra Palace, August 1936

Above: John Logie Baird's original television model built in 1926

Left: Sir John Reith became General Manager of the British Broadcasting Company in 1923 and was appointed Director General when the company was incorporated under Royal Charter in 1927. He left the BBC in 1938

Above: This photograph of a set in Studio B at Alexandra Palace shows how heavily early television borrowed from the conventions of theatre design, using a backcloth and curtained wings

Right: Bernard Hepton recalls, 'One of the responsibilities of the studio manager was to give the right cues for entrances and exits, sound effects, whatever.' Studio manager Eric Boseley calls actors to their marks, December 1938

WEDNESDAY JULY 7 VISION 45 Mc/s
THURSDAY JULY 8 SOUND 41.5 Mc/s

BRITISH MOVIETONEWS

'DERBY DAY'
Comic Opera by A. P. Herbert
Music by Alfred Reynolds
Bones............. Frank Drew
Bitter...... Frederick Ranalow
.... Tessa Deane
Bones......... Charlotte Leigh
lorace Waters, J.P.. George Baker
Waters...... Esther Coleman
.... Gordon Little
and
ra Robson, Christine Lindsay,
and Desmond Davis
he BBC Television Orchestra
Leader, Boris Pecker
Conductor, Hyam Greenbaum
Section of the BBC Chorus
and
or Anthony, Edward Crowther,
glas Ward, and D. Roderick Jones
roduced by Stephen Thomas

CLOSE

*All programme timings
shown on these pages
are approximate*

IZABETH FRENCH
bert Farjeon to be given on
ay night

Wednesday

3.0 'BETWEEN OURSELVES'
John Byron
Patricia Leonard
Patricia Russell
and
The Charlot Starlets
with
Dennis van Thal
and Bob Probst
Presentation by Reginald Smith

This will be another intimate floor
show of the type Reginald Smith
excels at presenting. All the artists
to be seen today have been associated
with that great figure of the revue
world, André Charlot, and all have
appeared in television in the past.
The Starlets are a troupe of eight,
picked by Charlot as likely candidates
for stardom. They first performed
at Alexandra Palace on May 5. A
feature of this show is that there
will be no band, all the music being
played on two pianos by Dennis
van Thal and Bob Probst, an entertaining combination that viewers have
seen on previous occasions.

3.20 BRITISH MOVIETONEWS

3.30 PICTURE PAGE
(Sixty-Ninth Edition)
A Magazine Programme
of General and Topical Interest
Edited by CECIL MADDEN
Produced by ROYSTON MORLEY
The Switchboard Girl : JOAN MILLER

4.0 CLOSE

9.0 'BETWEEN OURSELVES'
John Byron
Patricia Leonard
Patricia Russell
and
The Charlot Starlets
with
Dennis van Thal
and Bob Probst
Presentation by Reginald Smith

9.20 GAUMONT BRITISH
NEWS

9.30 PICTURE PAGE
(Seventieth Edition)
A Magazine Programme
of General and Topical Interest
Edited by CECIL MADDEN
Produced by ROYSTON MORLEY
The Switchboard Girl : JOAN MILLER

10.0 CLOSE

DR. A. C. JORDAN of the Men's Dress Reform Party who will
introduce a display of men's clothes on Tuesday night at 9.0. He is
seen here in two of his novel suits.

Thursday

3.0 Excerpts from
'RELACHE'
Ballet by Picabia
Music by Erik Satie
Choreography by Anthony Tudor
The BBC Television Orchestra
Leader, Boris Pecker
Conductor, Hyam Greenbaum
Presented for television by
Dallas Bower

This ballet, an experiment in ultra-
modernism, was performed by the
Swedish Ballet under Rolf de Maré
at the Théâtre des Champs-Elysées in
1924. Picabia, who was responsible
for nearly the whole production,
explained his work with : ' Life, life
as I like it, life without a moral, the
life of today, everything for today,
nothing for yesterday, nothing for
tomorrow, motor head-lights, pearl
necklaces, the rounded and slender
forms of women, publicity, music,
motor-cars, men in evening dress,
movement, noise, play, clear and
transparent water, the pleasures of
laughter—that is *Relâche.*'
More prosaically, *Relâche* has been
described as an instantaneous ballet
in two acts and a cinematographic
entr'acte. There are three main
characters, called simply the man,
the other man, and the woman.
There is little logical sequence in
the action, and altogether the whole
production is just the sort of thing
with which Satie and his disciples
delighted themselves and horrified
the uncomprehending.
In this short television presentation
it is impossible to give the whole
ballet, but it is hoped that the extracts
will give viewers an idea of the
complete work.

3.20 GAUMONT BRITISH
NEWS

3.30 GREER GARSON
and
D. A. CLARKE-SMITH
in
' HOW HE LIED TO HER
HUSBAND '
by George Bernard Shaw

This performance is particularly
interesting, as it is the first Shaw
play to be televised from Alexandra
Palace. *How He Lied to Her Husband,*
written more than thirty years ago,
is the only play that Shaw has allowed
to be seen in the cinema. The film
was directed by Cecil Lewis, who,
before going to Hollywood for the
filming of his war book, was a
television producer.
Both Greer Garson and D. A.
Clarke-Smith have had experience of
playing Shavian parts. One of
Greer Garson's first rôles on the
professional stage was that of the
patient in *Too True to be Good,* and
theatre-goers will remember D. A.
Clarke-Smith as Bonnington in *The
Doctor's Dilemma.*

4.0 CLOSE

9.0 'RELACHE'
(Details as at 3.0)

9.20 BRITISH MOVIETONEWS

9.30 'HOW HE LIED TO HER
HUSBAND'
(Details as at 3.30)

10.0 CLOSE

Television programmes on offer for Wednesday 7 July 1937

Right: The producer, vision mixer and assistant at work in the control box high above the studio. Ian Carmichael makes the point that, 'comparing the control rooms then to the ones they have now is a bit like comparing the Sopwith Camel with Concorde!'

Below: The Grove Family, television's first ever soap, ran from 1954 to 1957 and showed an ordinary family dealing with fundamental social issues. It was so popular that letters simply addressed to 'Gran, London', would find their way to actress Nancy Roberts (*seated right*)

1962

"THE MORTIMER TOUCH" BY ERIC LINKLATER   (PROJECT NO. SC62/1108)

REHEARSALS:

Kelvinside Church Hall, Glasgow.

Wednesday, 1st to Friday, 3rd August:	10.00a.m. - 5.00p.m.
Monday, 6th to Friday, 10th August:	10.00a.m. - 5.00p.m.
Monday, 13th to Wednesday, 15th August:	10.00a.m. - 5.00p.m.

Springfield Road Studio:
Thursday, 16th August: 10.00a.m. - 12.00p.m.

CAMERA REHEARSAL FOR ACT II (pp. 29/53: Scenes 18/41)

Springfield Road Studio, Glasgow.

Thursday, 16th August:	2.00p.m. - 5.00p.m.
Friday, 17th August:	10.00a.m. - 5.00p.m.
TAPING:	7.00p.m. - 8.00p.m. (VT/T/GW490/MGW)

CAMERA REHEARSALS FOR TRANSMISSION:

Springfield Road Studio, Glasgow.

Saturday, 18th August:	10.00a.m. - 5.00p.m.
Sunday, 19th August:	10.00a.m. - 5.00p.m.
	6.00p.m. - 8.00p.m.
TRANSMISSION:	8.45p.m. - 10.00p.m. NATIONAL NETWORK.

PRODUCER:	Mr. Stephen Harrison.
DIRECTOR:	Mr. Leonard Lewis.
PRODUCTION ASST:	Mr. John McRitchie
A.F.M	Miss Janet Hoenig.
FLOOR ASST.	Mr. James Sleigh.
SECRETARY:	Miss Dorothy Muir.
COSTUME SUPERVISOR:	Miss Kirstie Colam.
MAKEUP SUPERVISOR:	Miss Anne Donnelly.

Director Leonard Lewis had stills of *The Mortimer Touch,* shown here with the production's rehearsal schedule, photographed directly from the television screen. This was the only way of achieving a permanent record of the show

'Evening all': Arthur Rigby, Peter Byrne and Jack Warner in *Dixon of Dock Green*, broadcast from 1955 to 1976, still the longest-running police series ever to be shown on British Television

Colin Welland as PC David Graham in the police series *Z Cars*, a seminal example of hard-edged, authentic television drama that launched the careers of directors Ken Loach and John McGrath, and actors Stratford Johns, Frank Windsor, Brian Blessed, James Ellis and many others

Sean King, Ray Brooks, Stephen King and Carol White in *Cathy Come Home*. Written by Jeremy Sandford for *The Wednesday Play* series in November 1966, it ushered television drama into a new era of gritty realism

monitor and knocking him over like ninepins. A lot of things went on that people had to recover from and try and make it look good.' Phillip Manikum also recalls how cameras could harm the actors: 'A performer called Ray Barrett was acting his heart out in a play when his shoelace became tangled up in the camera wheel. As the camera moved for a close up it reeled Barrett in, dragging him across the studio floor until he hit the lens with a smack and disappeared . . . but the show went on!'

According to Malcolm Farquhar, the powers that be were single-minded in their handling of an injury if it occurred during live transmission. 'I did a rather complicated play written for television, with five sets dotted all over the studio. On one particular occasion the girl who was having the scene with me had to be in the next one too and she left me as I said my last speech. The next moment there was a terrible crash and she tripped over a cable and we thought she had broken her ankle. She couldn't move. They got her up and someone put a hand over her mouth so she couldn't scream. In the mean time they managed to do a shot of someone else and word came through that she would carry on but that she would be sitting in a chair. It meant that in subsequent scenes we sometimes had to get down on our knees in order to be the same height as her for the two-shots. There was no respite; if anything happened that was it, on you went. She went to hospital afterwards, but in studio they were ruthless.'

Eileen Atkins recalls an uncomfortable moment during *The Age of Kings*. 'The first half of the series was live then they switched to recording them, but when I played Jeanne D'Arc it was live. I was to be burned at the stake in the studio. There was a lot of discussion of how I should burn, with flames licking round me, and when it came to be broadcast, one of the people in the crowd must have really not liked me, because he kept throwing faggots on, slamming these logs against my shins, and I couldn't say stop. By the end my shins were bleeding.'

Glyn Houston also came to grief being burned at the stake. 'I played Captain John Smith in *The Pocahontas Story*. As they were burning me at the stake I said to the girl playing Pocahontas, who'd never done television before, "When you come to untie my hands, they won't really be tied, I'll just be holding them together, so you don't have to use the knife to saw through the rope. You just have to mime it because the camera is on the front of us." But come the live broadcast, I felt her sawing into the rope and she cut my hand very badly; in fact I dropped the rope with a yell, as you can imagine, and they thought it was very good acting. I finished the last few minutes with blood pouring out of my hand.'

Nigel Hawthorne recalled another 'burning' incident, from *Hurrah for Halloween*: 'There were some witches in it, one of whom was Joan Sims. She had to leap around a cauldron in which, because they didn't have dry ice in those days, they put some burning hemp. It choked everybody and during the actual transmission there were people gasping and coughing.' Peggy Mount was caught up in an even more spectacular conflagration: 'I did something called *The Cabin in the Clearing*; it was a cowboys-and-Indians thing. We were doing our nuts acting. Shaun Sutton was playing my husband. Off camera someone had to fire a [burning] arrow into a load of muck, because it had got to look as though we were on fire. Well, he missed and set fire to the set. We were acting away with smoke billowing around us.' Shaw Taylor, veteran presenter of *Police Five*, was another member of the cast and his account vividly conveys the drama of the event. 'At one point, one of my badly aimed fire arrows hit the thatch and set fire to the cabin for real, and Shaun Sutton, muttering unheard obscenities about myopic Indians, bravely beat out the flames with his coonskin hat, while Peggy Mount swung from his legs like a demented bell-ringer. The Chief Fire Officer was delayed from hitting Shaun in the mutton chops with a jet from the fire extinguisher only by the sight of Peggy Mount (off camera, thank heavens) falling to the ground clutching her spouse's buckskin trousers while Shaun, flailing at the fire with his badly singed coonskin, had only his doeskin jacket and Y-fronts for protection. But it was *live* – that was the joy of it, that was the challenge. For some twenty-seven minutes or so we held the youth of Britain enthralled.'

But events could take an altogether more serious turn. Actor and director Leslie Lawton recalls, 'There was a play called *The Pier*, which was Alan Bates's first television, about a group of Teddy boys on Brighton Pier. There was a flick-knife fight and somebody actually got stabbed.' Another grave incident is described by script writer Dick Sharples: 'In one episode of *Emergency Ward 10*, which was the original medical soap opera, started by ATV in 1956, they were using one of those heart-stimulation machines and they switched it on too high. They didn't save a bloke from a heart attack, they gave him one, and he sued and won. What they do now if they kill a bloke during recording, they can recast him, but then it was all live.'

Glyn Houston remembers watching television the night a real fatality occurred. 'My brother Donald was doing a live television in which he played a member of a group escaping after a bomb had been dropped on London. These five people were escaping in the underground to some sort of safety. I was watching it on television and suddenly there were only four people. There was no explanation as to where the fifth had gone. What transpired was that the fifth actor had had a heart attack. They had to carry on, but they knew the fellow had collapsed and when the show finished they were told that he was dead. My brother went to his mother with condolences.' Further insight into this tragic event is given by Peter Bowles, who actually appeared in the programme. 'I was in a production, very tragic and extraordinary in that it was live, of a play called *Underground* directed by Ted Kotcheff. It wasn't a big cast. Andrew Cruickshank was in it, and Donald Houston, and myself, and an actor called Gareth Jones. He was young, a Welsh actor, I believe he was in his twenties. He was rather portly and just beginning to make a name for himself. We rehearsed it in London and we all travelled up to Birmingham to transmit it, because that's what you used to do. It was about the atomic bomb falling on London and this particular group of people had gone into the underground in order to survive. There was a tremendous amount of rubble on set and because of this they had a doctor and a nurse on hand in case somebody broke their ankle. There was a tunnel linking one platform with another – Baker Street with Euston or whatever it was. Extraordinarily enough, as I remember it, Gareth was playing a character with heart trouble, and was seen to take pills occasionally, as the character in the course of the play. During transmission a little group of us was talking on camera while awaiting the arrival of Gareth Jones's character, who had some information for us. We could see him coming up towards us and he was going to arrive on cue, but we saw him drop, we saw him fall. The cameras were still turning, it was live. We had no idea what had happened, but he certainly wasn't coming our way. We could see people tending to him. The actors, including me, started making up lines: "I'm sure if So-and-so were here he would say . . ." Then they stopped the show for the adverts and I always remember Ted Kotcheff coming on to the floor and shouting, "What the hell is going on?" We were told that the actor had fallen and hurt himself, whereas in fact they knew that he was dead, he had had a heart attack. It was dreadful. He was a very close friend of Donald Houston's and it became quite apparent after the show that if they had told us he was dead, Donald would not have been able to continue. He was in a terrible state. It was an extraordinary experience, left indelibly on all of us, because somehow the show stumbled on.'

Such tragic events could not reasonably be foreseen, but there are other potential hazards against which actors are clearly warned. Every actor knows the adage, 'Never work with children or animals.' Several contributors to this book came unstuck in productions involving animals, and dogs in particular. Geoffrey Bayldon had to work with one in *Brass Band Comedies* by Willis Hall, which was broadcast first on the radio from Birmingham and then later done on television. 'The greyhound more than misbehaved itself, it had acute diarrhoea – the pong was unbelievable.'

Peggy Mount showed that incontinent cats could disgrace themselves just as well as dogs: 'In one episode [of *The Larkins*] we had six cats and six cat women – if you can imagine anything worse than six cat women you must tell me. One of the cats disappeared and everybody was off looking for it. Then we were on the air to a million people and Ronan O'Casey had a cat in his arms and he hated cats and the cat knew it. He scratched him badly and the blood was pouring out of Ronan and I went and took it from him and there was blood everywhere. The man playing the lead had to take the cat from me and the cat didn't like that and he shat all over him.'

Hilary Mason demonstrates that animals do not have to go to such extremes to steal a scene. 'I was in a children's play called *Gamble For a Throne*, set in the time of the Roundheads and the Cavaliers. Two actors, father and son, were having a discussion, very serious, it was. At the very last minute the director thought it would be nice to have a large dog lying in front of the fire while they were talking. It was an enormous dog and it sat there for a long time while they were talking, then suddenly it got up and sat down in between them, and it was the same size as they were! It was listening intently to them, inclining its head first towards one, then the other. They could hardly speak for laughing.'

Alec McCowen was another victim of canine caprice. 'One play we did there was a pond with live ducks on it in the studio and in the course of a scene somebody had to walk a dog past. We didn't have the animals before the day itself, and when we did it, the dog started to chase the ducks all over the place. The scene after that, I had to go into my

office and sit at my desk, and there on the desk was a duck!'
Margaret Tabor, who worked as a stage manager, recalls
having problems with a goat. 'In a production of *Cry, the
Beloved Country* they had goats as set-dressing and the goats
started to eat the set!'

Of all the actors who had to deal with the unpredictable
behaviour of animals, presenter David Jacobs probably
had the hardest time of it. 'I was the host of a quiz programme called *Make Up Your Mind*. We broadcast the programme live from the Granada studios in Manchester.
One week, for some reason or other, we had a live leopard
in the studios; it was trained to be sort of tame.
Unfortunately it was Manchester University Rag Week
and the boys and girls decided to rampage through the
studio. We had told everybody that even though the
leopard was on the end of the leash, everyone should be
perfectly calm, but when the students came rampaging
through the studio the leopard went berserk. It practically
had to be put down on the spot, but somehow or other the
trainer managed to control it. It was all over too quickly to
feel a sense of real danger, but it was very frightening.'

Even working with dead animals can pose problems for
the beleaguered actor, as Hilary Mason explains: 'In an
episode of *Z Cars* I played a sheep stealer's wife. It was a
filmed insert and we were driven to a knacker's yard in the
Chiltern Hills and I was told to go and look round the yard.
There were carcases hanging from the ceiling and pools of
liver and blood on the floor. The director said to me, "You
see that lorry over there, Hilary? You're going to run up the
tailboard of that lorry. You'll find two dead sheep inside;
pick up one of the dead sheep, sling it over your shoulder,

and run into the knacker's yard." You have no idea how heavy a dead sheep is. I did my best, but it was very heavy. The director was furious with me. He came running over, shouting, "Look as if you're used to it, dear." I had to do it again but the next one was a little bit lighter because it hadn't got a head!'

Faced with trials such as these, actors looked to one another for support, and many people spoke with warmth of the camaraderie that sustained them through the trauma of live broadcasts. Mary Kenton has happy memories: 'What used to happen is that you met at rehearsal. There was a long table in the rehearsal room and everybody sat round and the director introduced everyone. It was very nice because you all got to know each other, you had lunch together and you became a company.'

Trevor Bannister identifies the time permitted for rehearsal as a key element in the bonding process. 'You were all very reliant on each other – if somebody doesn't give you your cue then you're in trouble. It was very much a communal piece of work then. What you had then was a rehearsal period; you don't have a rehearsal period in television any more. You were able to get to know your fellow-actors and I think that improves the quality of the work. Once they went over to making television rather like films, you could be engaged to play a part and never meet other members of the cast because you don't have that essential rehearsal period, which was a very concentrated time. Now you can be in an episode of *Casualty* and your part constitutes one day's work.' Bannister's view is echoed by Glyn Houston. 'It was more like rehearsing for a play and it was very enjoyable. I was never happy with filming.

You'd get on a set with a big Hollywood star – I've worked with Clark Gable, Lana Turner, Victor Mature and so on – and you couldn't go up and say, "Let's run through this bit, Clark." You did your bit and that was what you were paid for.'

Peter Byrne thinks the *bonhomie* extended well beyond the cast members to include the technicians as well. 'On *Dixon of Dock Green* we had three different crews and they would stay together as the series went on and on, so we all knew each other and were interested in each other's work. It was a tremendous feeling of comradeship and every-body learning. We only meet each other now at memorial services, but there's still such a close bond.'

Newcomers to the profession, however, could feel unsure of their ground. According to Janet Hargreaves, 'There was a little bit more of a hierarchy then. I don't mean people were nasty to me, but I did know my place.' James Grout describes how he dealt with his first nerve-racking appearance opposite one of the great actors of his day. 'Wilfred Lawson used to challenge you, the first time he met you he would challenge you. I caught on to this. If you gave way to the challenge he could be quite a bully. I had to rush into the police station to find my wife, who had tried to drown herself in a canal. (It was a very happy sort of show!) The director knew that the best idea was to use Wilfred in short sharp bursts, so he wasn't at the read-through; he came after we started plotting. We were doing his scene and I came rushing on and said my line and he just stopped and he looked at me and he said, "Who the bloody hell are you?" He knew that I was unknown, that I hadn't done much television. I said, "My name is James

Grout, you drunken old sod!" I thought, *That's done it, I'm either in or I'm out*. There was a pause and then he laughed and came over and hugged me.'

Laughing (known in the business as 'corpsing') was common when television was broadcast live – most of it no doubt a by-product of the tremendous amount of stress participants were under. The most excruciating example of this is provided by Christopher Lee. 'About fifty years ago I was under contract to Rank and I was pushed into a programme called *Kaleidoscope*. I had to play a commissioner of French police, or something vaguely along those lines, and I had a scene with another actor who was playing an inspector of police. It nearly finished my career. The only way I could get on to the set was by standing in the corridor behind the stage, looking through a peephole. My cue was when he put the telephone down. I had to walk in and haul him over the coals. I walked in and before I had said a word he broke wind – I think that's the polite phrase. It was like a thunderclap, it was an absolute fusillade. It certainly took the wind out of my sails, but it put it into his. It went on, that was the awful thing. He was very nervous, the sweat was pouring down his face. I could see all the crew with handkerchiefs stuffed in their mouths, doubled over, tears streaming, trying not to make any noise while this man kept up this drumbeat. It was sheer terror on his part and it wasn't made any better by the fact that my line was "We shall have to do better" . . . We got through it but at that time I said, "Never ever, ever, ever again will I do live TV."'

On rare occasions, when seasoned performers were confident about what was required of them, a fit of corpsing could be induced on purpose. 'As we got blasé we started playing jokes on each other,' reveals Colin Welland. 'Brian Blessed finished a scene in Z Victor 1 and knew that Jimmy Ellis and I would be in there next, and he let off a stink bomb, and we had to do our whole scene in this terrible pong. As soon as it was over Jimmy had a scene off. He said, "I'll get him for this!" and raced up to the bar, grabbed a soda syphon, raced back down and lay underneath the camera lens and while Blessed was acting away, doing a big scene, he squirted in his trousers with soda water. There was no vindictiveness in all of this; it was a way of keeping the vitality, it stopped you getting stale.'

6

Calling the Shots

A PERSON WHO is 'calling the shots' is in overall charge of
proceedings. The phrase certainly applies to working practices in the early days of live television, when either the
director or the vision mixer called out the camera shots –
'Cut to camera two, cut to camera four' – thus defining
what the viewer at home would be looking at. This job was
carried out in the control room or gallery, and is described
in an early edition of the *Radio Times*:

> He [the producer] sits aloft in the control room with a bird's eye
> view of the studio from the observation window. In front of him
> are two monitors, one showing the image being transmitted and
> the other showing the image that can, if necessary, be transmitted
> from any of the other cameras. Behind him is the mixer, an engin-
> eer who has controls that fade out one camera and substitute
> another, an operation that is done at the producer's direction. On
> the producer's desk is a microphone that can put him in telephonic
> communication with the cameramen, who wear headphones.

The actor and director Bernard Hepton comments that
'In a gallery there is an awful lot to look at. If there are six

cameras on the floor there are six screens to look at, then there is the master to look at as well.' Ian Carmichael makes the point that 'Comparing the control rooms then to the ones they have now is a bit like comparing the Sopwith Camel with Concorde.'

Before the war the term 'producer' was largely used for the hands-on, artistic work that is now the director's remit. This is the case in the quotation from the *Radio Times* above. In the post-war period the industry began to adopt the job description used in the American film business, where the producer masterminded the production but the director was in artistic control of it. Leonard Lewis worked as first a director and then a producer and is well qualified to make the distinction between the two: 'The producer is the admiral and the director is the captain . . . he is driving the ship along and the producer cannot tell him how to drive the ship, he has got to leave him to it. Another thing we used to say was that if you were a producer people came to you with their problems, if you were a director they came to you with solutions. In the days of *Z Cars* if you were the director you would meet the writer, you would discuss the scripts, the writer would do rewrites for you. The ethos was that the writing was important and you were encouraged to do what the writer wanted. Later on the reverse happened: producers wanted to keep the writers to themselves, they didn't want the director coming along. More and more these days producers have a colossal influence over the whole thing.' Eve Pearce agrees: 'Directors in those days were very much more influential than they are now. It is producers who are influential now, not directors. Directors have lost power, enormously. It's about money. The idea was that the producer would stop things rollicking out of control, but now they have a say over whether they've got the right actor and so on. It's like America.'

Bernard Hepton was another who worked both as director and producer and he also attempts to clarify the difference in the work they do. 'A lot of people don't understand the difference between producer and director. The producer gets the thing on. If it's his baby, he actually gets the thing written and then finds the director to do it. The director is directly responsible to the producer, but if the producer has done his job well then the director has a very free hand, but the person responsible for a total success or failure is the producer. If it's a success it's usually the director and the actors who get the plaudits and if it's a failure it's always the producer who gets kicked up the backside.'

Actors tended to have more contact with the director, who oversaw them at rehearsals, rather than the producer, who was often a more remote figure. Of the contributors to this book, only two made reference to a producer and in each case it was Sidney Bernstein, the impresario who founded Granada. Eve Pearce remarks, 'Sidney Bernstein ran Granada, he really ran it, he was a hands-on man. If he didn't like the tie you were planning to wear on screen, he would tell you to go and change it.'

In the early days most directors were poached from the theatre and, like the performers, were thrown in at the deep end. Ian Carmichael started his career as a stage and film actor before becoming a television performer, and after a few years of working in light entertainment he was made an offer he found difficult to refuse. 'In the late forties the BBC was very short of directors, or producers as they were called then, and Michael Mills put my name forward. He said, "I can get you a fifteen-minute slot in about six weeks' time; you're only allowed to use one artist." The umbrella title of these slots was *Starlight*. I said, "Michael, hold the line, I've never been up in a producer's box in my life, I wouldn't know what to do, I don't know anything about cameras." He offered to do the first one with me and the second one sitting behind watching while I did it. For the third I would be on my own. I picked Petula Clarke. On the day of rehearsal I got there, Petula got there, her pianist got there, the cameras got there – and there was no sign of Michael. I thought, *Bloody hell!* I waited a good half-hour, but I could not afford to wait any longer, so I climbed up the vertical ladder into the control box for the first time in my life and sat in front of two television screens. There was a technical man behind me who helped me a bit. Michael blew in after I had run it through once, saying, "Carry on, keep going," and sat behind me while we ran it a second time. Then he got up, moved to the door of the control room and said, "Right, that's fine, I'll give you a ring tonight to let you know how it went!" '

Leonard Lewis was another who was left to sink or swim. 'I applied for a holiday-relief post and got one working as an AFM for BBC Drama. When I started I thought it was a bit of a doddle: you didn't have to work nearly as hard as you did in the theatre. You had people to do things for you, you didn't have to do it all yourself. At first I was a bit wary but after a while it got me hooked. Then I became a production assistant and because I wanted to be a director I used to ask permission to sit in the box behind whoever was directing and watch the transmission. As a production assistant I worked on a show where the director had a nervous breakdown the week before transmission. I had to take over. It wasn't a good show but I got it on the air without disgrace. As a result of that I was allowed to direct *Z Cars* and I eventually became a staff director.'

Eve Pearce remembers, 'In 1956 Granada was the only independent television company that had a director's course.' Bernard Hepton benefited from similar training offered by the BBC. 'In 1962 I was lucky enough to be taken on by the BBC and trained as a director and producer. One of the most interesting things that was said on that course was "Do not forget that when you put something out on television you are not playing to an audience of millions, you are playing to one person in a room." It gives you a different sort of slant on what your audience actually is. They tried to inculcate in us a real sense of responsibility and it showed in the productions. Programmes like *Cathy Come Home* showed a sense of right and wrong, of civic responsibility.'

In a *Radio Times* column called 'News For Televiewers' an early aspect of the director's work is described: 'Every producer begins his plans for a show by sketching a camera plan, a drawing rough enough to make a draughtsman wince, but accurate enough to show the approximate positions of the cameras in the studio. This plan is approved and occasionally altered by the production manager, delivered to the studio engineer and distributed amongst the cameramen.' Once the production team agreed on such essentials, rehearsals began; the actor Brian Murphy recalls what they were like. 'You rehearsed for two weeks, much as you would in a theatre. The director said, "We're working out the play and the people in it. I'll shoot it when we get to the studio." In other words, rehearsals weren't hampered by camera shots. Later on directors started to view rehearsals as a chance for lining up their shots, rather than sometimes doing the play. We'd be in the studio for two to four days and we'd be shot by four cameras.'

The pioneering television director George More O'Ferrall also saw the performance in terms of theatre. In an article for the *Radio Times* he wrote: 'The television producer is directly in control of his medium during performance. He is part of the performance in a way that a stage producer or a film director can never be . . . Not only can one correct small errors of production but – what is more important – one can take full advantage of the actors' performance, for television acting differs from screen acting in that it is a sustained performance as in the theatre.' He goes on to say:

I believe that television drama is a medium of its own and that it is a mistake to try to copy the films. We should regard fine acting as our chief asset and use the cameras to show it to its best advantage, and, where possible, to heighten its effect. The value of the close-up is immeasurable . . . although the television producer's studio work is closely allied to that of a film producer, it is essential that he should have a real knowledge of the theatre. To his sense of tempo and rhythm in acting he must add correct tempo and rhythm in the tracking and panning of his cameras and a faculty for deciding in a split-second the exact moment to mix to another camera in order to give greater dramatic value.

The actor Harry Landis speaks for many when he says, 'The best directors are those who have been theatre directors as well, because a theatre director talks about what the play is about and how the characters fit into the jigsaw of the author's intention. He knows how to make the point of the play, how to approach that artistically, and all the time he's keeping an eye on the acting and guiding it. A television director is trained to be technical because he has to know about the cables on the cameras – they have to work out the shots so that the cameras don't cross. Rather like plumbers, they are trained in the niceties of technical bits and pieces and if they are intelligent they will know about the play. I find there is a great difference between the two types. Actors are much more sympathetic to the theatre directors because they can talk about the particular problems in a given scene. If you wanted to talk about a problem to a director whose background was only in telly they would say, "Say it fast and get it over with."' Ian Flintoff shares Landis's view: 'There used to be much more discussion about the work. Nowadays, on the whole, directors seem to trust the actors enormously. They expect you to turn up and be competent and know what you're doing. In the sixties television used to be much closer to the theatre; you would talk about the motivation of a scene, the motivation of a role, the actuality of a character. At that time many of the directors and nearly all the actors came from the theatre, so unsurprisingly they brought the idiom of the theatre into the television studio. There was something very satisfying about that from the actor's point of view.'

Perhaps directors' attention had to be spread too thinly for them to nurture their companies as much as they would in the theatre. Peggy Mount observed that 'The director's main function was putting it on and photographing it well. The rest of it was up to us. We gave him the material that he needed. From his point of view it was far more technical than any stage play.' Leonard Lewis outlines some of the preoccupations that used to beset him: 'As a director in television I had some of the most exciting, adrenalin-pumping times you can imagine. As a director you were not only in charge of what shot you wanted (which you planned beforehand on your camera script, you couldn't do it on the hoof); you also had to cue the actors, put the sound effects on and in a live performance you were responsible for speeding up or slowing down in order to make the deadline on time. There was a certain amount of leeway, but even so Presentation, who were running the network, would be on the phone constantly – how was it running? They needed to know how it was running in rela-tion to the timing of the dress rehearsal. In something like *Z Cars* you might have fifty, sixty, seventy or even sometimes eighty scenes in a fifty-minute broadcast. I used to memor-ise the script. You used to say to Presentation, "It's running at such and such a time," and ten minutes before the end you would tell them, "We will finish at such and such a time." All the while you were checking with your assistant, who was on the stopwatches. She would say, "We are thirty seconds ahead of where we were in the dress run." You had little tricks. If you were running telecine [filmed inserts], telecine ran on an eight-second cue so you had to run it eight seconds before you needed it at the end of a scene. If you ran it just a tiny bit early you could save a second, or if you ran it a little bit late, you could add a second. Telecine was the film that you shot on location, which you could edit. It was a bit primitive in terms of communication too. You would shout your instructions and you had a man standing by your side who was the technical manager with a phone to telecine. You might lose the line or they might not be able to hear you.'

Many performers hated the fact that, if something went wrong, the director on whom they depended for leadership was trapped beyond reach in the gallery. Faith Brook remarks, 'After at least two weeks' rehearsal we went into the studio and the director promptly disappeared into the control room and became a disembodied voice. If there was a real cock-up on the floor he'd make his way down and try to sort it out.' James Grout explains why they so rarely appeared: 'I used to think it was such a silly system that the director sat up there in the gallery when we really needed him. You had a very close relationship, but the directive from above was that they stayed in their control box, because every time they came down from it on to the studio floor to sort something out, it took something like three and a half minutes just to physically make the journey. If they did this four or five times, sixteen minutes were wasted. Studios cost I don't know how many pounds a minute to run, so it made sense. A few of the directors ignored it, they were the very clever ones who sort of had a letter from Mother, so nobody dared to approach them.' David London, who worked as a floor manager, corroborates this. 'When programmes were live, because of the shortage of time the director would stay upstairs in the control box and you would stay on the floor and if he wanted something done you would do it for him. Once they were able to record, directors suddenly started wanting to have more communication with the artists, so they'd come down on the floor . . . Because they could use tape in the same way they could use film, directors started becoming film directors on tape on the floor. Now it's common practice.'

Leonard Lewis recalls the moment when he realized how tough it would be to direct: 'I once went to watch a live *Z Cars* and it was one where things went wrong – cameras and booms were in shot, things just got out of kilter. I sat up in the gallery watching this disaster and I realized that the people in front of me who were running the show hadn't realised it was happening. The director was watching his script and listening to what was going on; the assistant was calling the shots and again her eyes were down on her script; the vision mixer was watching her preview monitor instead of another one; and the technical manager, who might otherwise have spotted it, was on the phone to somebody. It made me think that when I was a director I would never take my eyes off the screen, and by and large I achieved that, but it meant that you had to learn the script first. If you had been in rep and had been learning plays week after week, it wasn't that difficult.'

Barbara Lott recalls her husband, the director Stuart Latham (who was known as Harry), getting off to a sticky start. 'Harry's first job was to direct *The Noble Spaniard* by Somerset Maugham. It started off with a middle-aged man having a very long speech and Harry cast an actor he was terribly fond of called Lloyd Pearson. At the transmission Lloyd Pearson came on, said his first two lines and then dried stone dead. Being a good stage actor he cut to the next cue, so all Harry's cameras were in the wrong position. He said, "My first instinct was to stand up and leave the building, but as I stood up the producer's hand clamped on my shoulder and pulled me back!" '

Writer Dick Sharples recalls that Ronald Baxter was given an unnecessarily hard blooding: 'Ronnie Baxter's first show as a director was with the comedian Jimmy James, who was a very funny man. He had a group of feeds surrounding him. Ronnie was very nervous. About an hour before transmission, one of the sidekicks, a tall, gaunt fellow called Bretton Wood, came up to Ronnie and he said, "I don't know how to tell you this, it's Jimmy . . ." "What's the matter?" "He's totally pie-eyed; it's his nerves you see, he gets very nervous indeed." Ronnie said, "Oh my God, what are we going to do? We're going out live, we've got an audience out there. What the hell are we going to do?" Bretton said, "Don't worry, we'll wing it." "For a whole hour?" Ronnie stormed into Jimmy's dressing room and Jimmy was sitting there with a bottle of beer, drunk. Ronnie said, "We're going to have to wing it." He raced down to the studio, the rolling credits were going, then the opening credits, and they went into the show. And of course Jimmy didn't miss a trick, he was perfect. Afterwards the crew said to Ronnie, "Didn't you know, he's teetotal!" '

A number of directors did however seek solace, according to Miriam Karlin: 'One thing that a lot of the directors suffered from, and it was because it was such a tense time, they all used to get pissed in the bar afterwards. There was a lot of alcoholism around. There has always been a drinking culture at the BBC.'

*

One of the key players in the control box was the vision mixer, whose function is described by James Grout. 'Upstairs in the gallery was a poor devil known as the vision mixer; he was every bit as important as the director. He is the man who selects what camera view you see simply by pressing the button for that camera. At certain cues and places he would simply change the view. That cutting process is very much a part of the end product. Usually the cameramen and the director have worked out who is going to shoot what, but the vision mixer knows when these things are coming up.' Bernard Hepton offers further detail about these responsibilities: 'In the days of electronic [as opposed to digital] recording, there was always the very important post of vision mixer. The director used to make a camera script. Where there was a cut from one person to another he would put a very definite mark on the camera script. Everybody would look at the camera script to see which camera was going to do what, when. The vision mixer would follow the script and where the cut was he would call, "Camera four." There was a particular vision mixer who was a very experienced lady and she knitted all the time, watching the screen. If the director said, "Excuse me, the cut doesn't come there," she would say, "Oh yes, it's better there." She actually made the programme for the director and usually it was right. She was a very famous lady, looked on with awe.'

It is impossible to pay tribute to all the influential directors who so shaped the emergent medium, but a number of names recurred frequently during actors' reminiscences. Pioneer George More O'Ferrall is singled out for praise by fellow-director Dallas Bower: 'George More O'Ferrall probably contributed more to early television drama than any of us, his production of *Journey's End*, *Hamlet* and James Elroy Flecker's *Hassan* with the Delius incidental music being outstanding events in television's early history.' Other responses are more ambivalent. Richard Bebb recalled, 'Directors like Michael Barry and George More O'Ferrall were creating the language of television. George More O'Ferrall couldn't direct actors but he could direct cameras.' He seems to have had a peculiar attitude to this piece of apparatus, according to Barbara Lott: 'There was a story about George More O'Ferrall, who only ever used one camera and said, "I don't like to move it, it's bad for it."'

Another giant of the early days was Michael Barry, of whom Dallas Bowers says, 'After the war when he became head of television drama he was to have more influence on the development of live television drama than anyone.' Judy Campbell provides a detailed account of him: 'People always thought that he must be a judge or a bishop because he always looked so solemn. In actual fact he was the most friendly and sweet of men, but he had this solemn demeanour which meant that people didn't dare go up and ask him something when he was having his sandwiches because they thought his mind was on greater things. His mind *was* on greater things – he was always trying to solve some puzzle – but really he was very approachable. He was very, very good at his job. He was enormously thorough. That sounds a curious adjective, but in approaching this new medium he mastered it all. He thought it through, he knew where cameras should go, and he was also a good director as far as performances went. He knew where you should sit and where you should stand and the pace of the thing. He knew his stuff, so that you felt safe in his hands. He was a good administrator as well and it's a very rare combination, to have an artistic gift and to be able to administrate.'

Richard Bebb outlines Barry's instinctive grasp of the possibilities presented by television: 'In 1949 I wrote off to all the television directors and my letter had the good fortune to land on the desk of Michael Barry when he was looking for somebody to play the leading part in a play that he had written called *Promise of Tomorrow* . . . All the other television directors would never miss a Michael Barry production because he was always inventing new things. For example, for the scenes on the train all the moving effects were with a simple lighting gadget that he had invented. The language was fresh and created by brilliant people.' On a personal level, 'Michael Barry was mesmeric. He had very dark eyes; he was a deeply serious man without a great deal of humour, but total concentration. To feel his eyes on you in rehearsal was enormously challenging.' Barbara Lott gives recognition not just to Barry but also to his opposite number at ITV. 'There were two great men in the early days. There was Michael Barry at the BBC, and a man called Desmond Davies at ITV. They were both men of great perception and terribly good at their jobs.' ITV had other major talents in the directing field. One of the earliest recruits to independent television drama was Sydney Newman, who devised the *Armchair Theatre* format. Harry Landis comments that 'He brought a left-wing thrust with him and did away with plays with french windows. He featured real people and used writers like Alun Owen. The same revolution that happened in the theatre with Osborne and Wesker and Pinter happened in television with people like Sydney Newman. There was a kind of new wave in television and I was part of that.'

The *Armchair Theatre* series was indeed a landmark in television history. Not only did it establish the credentials of a new kind of 'kitchen sink' realism, with productions of an extremely high standard, according to Leonard Lewis it also provoked the BBC into a reassessment of its own work. 'When Sydney Newman started *Armchair Theatre* on ITV, the BBC realized they were becoming a bit fuddy-duddy and they brought in a lot of freelance directors, which meant that eventually there were only a few staff directors left.' Once the Corporation acknowledged the need to revitalize its own output, it concluded that the only person to achieve this effectively was Newman himself, and accordingly in the 1960s he moved across to the other side. Peter Byrne recalls, 'There were giants in charge of the BBC in the golden age during the sixties, when Carlton Greene was the Director-General. He was a great risk taker – *That Was the Week That Was*, *The Comedy Playhouse*. That spawned all those wonderful comedies – *Steptoe*, Alf Garnett. He brought over Sydney Newman from commercial television. Newman did daring things like shoot through a plant or through a window; he made the camera much more mobile.'

Bernard Hepton worked as a director under Newman at the BBC. 'The drama group was hellishly rebellious, wonderfully rebellious. They said, "Why can't we do this?" "Bugger it, I'm going to do it and I don't care if I go over budget or not." And they created magic. Those were the days when there wasn't this tremendous hoo-ha about ratings. It was the time when Sydney Newman was Head of Drama at the BBC. We used to call him "the Mexican bandit" because he looked exactly like a Mexican bandit. He was such a maverick that the BBC people couldn't quite contain him. There was a terrible silting-up between his office and the head office – nobody spoke to each other. He brought in young blood, bursting with ideas. The BBC people who had been there for an awfully long time felt themselves being terribly outpaced.'

Newman brought a number of colleagues to England with him, all of whom went on to carve successful careers. George Baker recollects, 'I did a play called *Domesday for Dyson* by J. B. Priestley. It was directed by Silvio Maritzano. He came over from Canada with Sydney Newman and Ted Kotcheff. He was a wonderful director; he knew his television and was very happy to tell you what to do and how to do it. He was an extraordinary man. I felt I had really begun to learn about television.'

There seem to have been a number of imported talents in television at this time, and the ability to attract people of international standing suggests that the medium in Britain was at the cutting edge. Miriam Karlin reminisces about working with the Russian director Tanya Levin: 'We had the read-through one day and by the second day she was already saying, "Find me, darling, find me." I told this to a director friend of mine, Lionel Harris, and he suggested that I went in and said, "I found you yesterday, now you find me." ' Leslie Lawton confirms Karlin's account: 'Tanya Levin was a wonderful Russian director who used to say, "Darling, I am the camera, I am the camera, follow me, follow me." One day in rehearsal Miriam Karlin stopped and said, "Right, that's it. It's my turn to be the camera. You fucking follow me." '

Husband and wife Roger Ostime and Hilary Mason both worked for Rudolf Cartier, who was 'extraordinary to work for. He was very Viennese,' according to Hilary. Roger remembers, 'He was very unpredictable; he had an autocratic style like an old film director.'

British directors could be eccentric too. Eve Pearce recalls a director at Granada called Derek Bennett. 'During the first week of rehearsal he used to spend the first half-hour of every day playing football. He thought that you had to be properly warmed up and then you'd be in good form. It was a good idea. The men loved it. The women didn't love it quite as much but he insisted that you didn't just sit and watch.' Alec McCowen describes another unusual practice: 'The director Stuart Burge had this ploy he used. On the day of transmission he always looked as though he was about to faint. He looked really dreadful, and so all the cast would want to pull out the stops to make it really good for him – "Stop Stuart faint-ing!" – and of course afterwards he'd be absolutely fine and all of us would be completely wrung out.'

Another crucial member of the creative team is the writer. Part of Sydney Newman's legendary success was his ability to discover and bring on great scriptwriters. But, as with all areas of production, the quality was varied. George Baker remembers working with 'writers like Giles Cooper, J. B. Priestley – an incredibly high standard', whereas Hilary Mason comments, 'You had to get used to the writing sometimes. The writing was sometimes poor stuff.'

Peggy Mount was able to convey what it was like to work with a writer over a sustained period of time. The series *The Larkins* ran from 1958 to 1964 and she was full of praise for Fred Robinson. 'With *The Larkins* we were very, very lucky. We had the most wonderful scriptwriter. He was a Scoutmaster and somebody read his Christmas show and sent it to the Grade organisation and said, "Give that to Peggy Mount." I didn't want to do another loud-voiced woman, but I read it and it was such a wonderful script.' She suggests that in a long-running programme the relationship was symbiotic. 'In terms of the development of the characters and the stories, the writer gathered what he wanted from us and worked on it.' In an aside, Mount remarked that writers sometimes failed to think things through from the actor's point of view. 'If you had to be in a summer dress here, then in a fur coat there, the script-writers never thought it through and you'd find yourself tearing round the studio throwing your clothes off.'

Leonard Lewis provides a director's perspective on the work of writers: '*Z Cars* was a very writer-dominated show. You would have a writers' meeting for every series. The writers would sit down and they would agree what the show was going to do. Because it was a serial, each episode was meant to be contained, it was individual stories, not a soap opera. Although the characters did change, it was the story that was important. What the writer wrote was what appeared on the screen, for the most part. Actors were not allowed to rewrite or paraphrase, directors were not allowed to have their directorial influence, the script was your bible. A certain amount of talking in the bar went on, but the actor's influence came from the screen. The writers saw their episodes being transmitted and saw the character of, say, Barlow in action and they said, "I can do more with this man." If the actors were very good then the writers would warm to them; it was a kind of osmosis. The reverse could happen too.'

Dick Sharples explains that the writer had to know his place. 'Some producers, directors and actors loved to have the writers around and I used to go to the read-through and I'd hang around on the first day and I'd say, "If anything is not working let me know. I'd prefer to rewrite it than the tea lady having a go." I kept a low profile; I wouldn't go and talk to the actors – there is only one boss on the floor and that's the director.' However, 'I felt very strongly about protecting the script, I really did. I had some horrific experiences with cowardly directors and incompetent script editors.'

Sharples compares the BBC and ITV: 'The BBC did coddle writers more. Even if the ratings were appalling for a first series they would recognize that there was something there and say, "Let's give it a chance to gel," and they would do another series. If two series failed then they would say, "It's time to take it off." With ITV, then and now, you had to hit the ratings straight off.' He looks back with nostalgia to the era of live broadcasts. 'Now there are so many script advisers, script consultants and committees, and everybody feels they have to put their sixpenny-worth in, so the creative people, the writers and directors, are being interfered with. It's become writing by numbers, with a checklist of things that should be in every script. It's very depressing. It reduces everything to a formula and formulas don't work.'

7

A Motley Crew

THE ARTISTIC VISION of the writers, producers and direct-ors, although expressed largely by performers, would have been unrealizable without the support of a cohort of expert technicians, known as the crew. These consisted of cameramen, sound engineers, lighting men, stage man-agers, props men, cable pullers etc., and were highly thought of by the artists. 'All the technicians, the camera-men, the wardrobe people, they were all wonderful,' says Miriam Karlin. Given the practical and artistic challenges that the early days of live television presented to the crews, Brian Murphy also believes the standard of achievement was high. 'It's surprising to me that there weren't more booms seen in pictures, or that the four or five cameras running around didn't bump into each other or get seen in shot more often.'

A number of interviewees spoke of the team spirit that prevailed. Margaret Tyzack remembers, 'There was a wonderful camaraderie about it all. There was a great link between the actors and the technicians that you don't get so much nowadays. In a sense they were holding on to you and you were holding on to them.' This theme is taken up by Judy Campbell: 'One had a great sense of camaraderie with the technicians, which I have never felt in a film studio. In films I didn't feel that the technicians were on my side, although they probably were. They always seemed to be in conference with the director and then you'd be told what to do, whereas in television you could make suggestions yourself and say, "Would it be a good idea if I came down these stairs a bit quicker?", and the technicians would ask for your help – "Could you help me by sitting a bit sideways so that I can get through here or avoid that?" Compared to this, in a film studio I felt rather disadvantaged and in awe of people.'

The director Leonard Lewis agrees that technicians were both involved and influential: 'In the early days of television the technicians had quite a say. A few days before the studio, they would come to the technical rehearsal. They would look at what you were doing and they would look at the plan and they would be very critical about what you were trying to do – "I can't get that shot." '

Although radio was the senior medium at the BBC, Barbara Lott thinks there was not much of a crossover from Broadcasting House to Alexandra Palace: 'I don't know whether radio technicians went into television. I think television technicians came from the theatre.' Certainly a significant number came from the stage and doubtless some, like Dallas Bower, from the world of the cinema. Whatever their origins, like the actors and directors before them, technicians often found themselves learning on the job. According to both Bernard Hepton and engineer Roy Glew, more often than not staff benefited from working in regional studios, where they learned the skills they needed. Hepton recalls, 'In an autonomous unit like the BBC in Birmingham they were able to bring on their own apprentices. I saw people start out as call boys, then they went on to vision-mixing, then they went on to all sorts of things – directors' and producers' assistants – then they went back to vision-mixing, then they went on the floor. They learned the business from every aspect.' Glew concurs: 'I was lucky because when I was a technical assistant I was sent to a region, where you had a chance to do everything. A lot of technical assistants who stayed in London only did engineering, but I operated the sound boom, which taught me an awful lot I never knew before. I also did the camera operation, not actually on the floor but what we used to call "racks", which was camera control . . . My London contemporaries never had the opportunity to work on outside broadcasts. When I came back to London and met up with the few people I'd been on the initial courses with, I found I'd got all this extra operational experience.'

One of the most important members of a television crew is the cameraman, and when Alexandra Palace first went on air there were ten of them employed. An early edition of the *Radio Times* describes how complex their job was:

Each camera has a viewfinder of ground glass, about four inches by five inches, which gives an inverted image. Here then is one difference: the cameraman sees everything upside down, chorus girls standing on their heads and tapping their feet on the ceiling, prima donnas looking like circus acrobats. Obviously the first requisite of the cameraman is a cool head. Three things often concern him at once: focusing, panning and composition. The focusing is manipulated by a control knob on either side of the viewfinder and the difficulty of doing this successfully in a Fred Astaire–Ginger Rogers type of dance scene can be imagined. As for composition, this is an important artistic consideration, in which the skilled photographer shows to advantage. The lighting tends to make things even more harassing. The illumination from the five kw lamps occasionally makes the image on the viewfinder rather indistinct.

The men who operated these machines were generally held in high regard. George Baker maintains that 'The BBC had some splendid cameramen who were very old-fashioned, and some extremely well-trained cameramen who were rather acceptable, and some of them were quite brilliant.' The actress Mary Kenton is full of praise for them: 'Photography has become so wonderful now, but it was very crude then. The cameramen were just wonderful, because it was a hell of a job. They were always so polite and helpful.' Harry Landis expands on this point: 'The people who got directors out of trouble often were the cameramen. There used to be a producer's run which the technicians went to and often after this they'd say, "You can't have me doing that two-shot after doing the close-up, because I won't be able to get round with the cables in the way."'

Even if they weren't overtly offering advice, they could perform a vital function for the actor, as Eve Pearce explains. 'I used to think that if you could get a response from the cameraman, that was the test. They were generous if they thought that you were doing something good, they would give you the thumbs-up. They took the place of the theatre audience and I would actually play to the cameraman. It's very difficult to play to all these millions and millions of people who may or may not be watching you, but he was there.' Another actor who emphasizes the importance of forming a good relationship with the cameraman is Leslie Lawton. 'The cameramen were just fantastic; they'd be waving you into a shot. You had one eye on the hand of the cameraman because that's how you got your directions. If you were sensible you made friends with them. Whoever was on number-one camera was virtually the director on the floor. You'd get their shots for them too, if you were in a two-shot and you could see that the other person was off their marks, you'd get the shot for them too' – by moving to a new position to help the cameraman keep both people in shot.

Peter Bowles is quick to sympathize with the cameramen who worked in live television. 'Actors on the whole like an adrenalin rush. Those who it seemed to affect most of all were the cameramen – their veins were standing out, they were sweating, they had most of the responsibility. They had these rather unwieldy large cameras which they had to push around; they had to move them very, very quickly from one set to another, they maybe had to cover twenty or thirty yards.'

The size of the cameras and the relative inexperience of those working with them meant that to begin with at Alexandra Palace they remained fairly static. 'The cameras were rigid,' says Judy Campbell. 'Moving the cameras came in later, I think. You could push them about, but they were simply enormous. So most plays were done with a camera at each corner – cameras one, two, three and four.' Maria Charles concurs: 'The camera didn't move too much; you moved. They weren't like they are now, they were great big lumbering things with lights on the side of them, like you see in old movies and things.'

According to Margaret Tyzack, 'There were no zoom lenses in those days, and if the director wanted a close-up then the camera came in so close to you that it sometimes ran over your feet.' Peter Byrne sustained this type of injury: 'If they wanted to come in to you, they would actually move in and sometimes run over your foot. You would keep going with the tears streaming down your cheeks. But you learned to cope with these things.' Even if you didn't suffer physically, being in close-up could unnerve an actor, as Malcolm Farquhar explains. 'The first thing that really frightened me sick, and a lot of other people, was the size of the cameras . . . When you were in close-up, this bloody great thing started to come towards you and ended up about three inches from your cheek. You've got to keep your head. I kept thinking as I was talking, *They can only see my lughole.* You were never warned when it was going to happen. They were learning their trade. You also had to watch for the red cue light, which was when you started the scene, it went off when the scene was finished. If your profile was in close-up you had no way of seeing the cue light, and you had to depend on a manual cue that they sometimes forgot.'

Maurice Denham describes how the technology evolved: 'Gradually, instead of one camera, they had one camera with two lenses, and then they had five lenses which could swivel round so that the camera could keep far away from you but could pick you up in close-up from a long way away.' The potential problems of working with such equipment are recalled by Michael Kilgarriff. 'The lenses weren't clever enough to focus so each camera had four of them, and one of the jobs of the cameraman was to change the lenses by swivelling them from long shot to mid-shot to close-up. If he turned the lens too quickly before he got the cue you used to see the picture go side-ways.'

Judy Campbell points out that in the event of a mishap there were always cameras on standby to step into the breach. 'If one of the cameras wasn't working, which quite often happened, they would point you to number-two camera, to indicate that you must turn round and play your scene over there.' This happened to Josephine Tewson: 'I had some boiled cabbage that I had to strain. I had to pour it into a colander and put it down. The camera was placed just outside the kitchen window. In those days if the red light was on that meant that camera was taking the picture. I suddenly realized there was something the matter – halfway through my big speech while I was strain-ing this stuff, the red light went off. I thought, *My God, what shall I do? Well, I'd better go on. I wonder if I ought to turn round in case there is another camera taking me from somewhere else.* I went on valiantly while they were busy taking the camera apart and mending it.'

Moving the cameras from long shot to close-up within a scene, and also from set to set inside the studio, was a logis-tical nightmare. Wendy Craig explains: 'It was very stress-ful for the cameramen. Their cables would get frightfully tangled up and sometimes they would be trapped in a corner when they were meant to be up at the other end of the studio. If you had four cameras and all the cables coming from them it was like spaghetti. They had cable pullers, they still have. It was a very responsible job to sort out the cables and make sure they were never twisted up, so that the cameraman could rush to his next venue.' In order to transmit a demonstration exhibition of the earliest form of television from the North London Exhibition in October 1936, six men were needed to control the Emitron camera cable, two men were used for the microphone cable, another two for the principal light cable, and a further two for the second light cable. The fact that twelve men were occupied in cable management alone helps to convey a sense of how congested the sets could become. James Grout confirms this impression: 'Everything was much bigger then than it is now. The cameras were huge; the cables connecting the cameras to the control box were about two inches thick, thicker than a man's wrist; sometimes there were thirty or forty yards of this stuff and they coiled it up when it wasn't needed – it looked like ship's rope. Cable-jumping became a great art, leaping up quite high mounds of this stuff and hoping you didn't slip.'

In addition to the mess, Peter Byrne says, 'The noise in the studio at that time stays with me. It was a swishing noise, because the motorized cameras used to have a man on the front who was seated, a chap behind him and a man behind him who was driving. The cameraman would wave his hand and he would control whether they moved to the left or the right. They were attached to very, very thick cables that were plugged into four terminals at different points in the room. When you were rehearsing, the directors had a ground plan and they attached different coloured pieces of cotton to the terminals on the ground plan . . . If the director hadn't done his homework properly they got tied up in a knot. It happened to me on one programme. There was a complete traffic jam and they had to unplug the cables and in the mean time cut to another set where the actors weren't ready and were picking their noses!'

The actor Peter Birrel recalls the consequence of one such entanglement. 'In the early sixties I was in an episode of a children's serial for Rediffusion TV (long deceased!) called *Frontier Drums*. I don't recall whether it was actually live – I think it was – or "as live" . . . so there was no stopping once the performance began. The driver who sat on the back of the big Vinton crane camera dolly managed to complete a whole circle and run over his own motor cable. There was a great flash and a bang and the studio filled with smoke. But of course we couldn't stop, so for the rest of the show several hefty men tried to push the big crane from position to position, though I doubt it got to many on time, while in the control box they were improvising the camera plot on the run. I never saw it (thank God!) but it must have been visually surreal.'

In order for the cameras and their operators to work effectively, the scenes they were photographing had to be properly lit. D. R. Campbell was in charge of lighting when Alexandra Palace opened and during a wartime broadcast he reminisced about the challenges involved: 'There was so little time for normal rehearsals. We put on a complete change of programme twice a day, and that meant lighting perhaps thirty different subjects or sets.' The biggest problem was 'Unnatural shadows. The human nose does not cast the most becoming shadow. And then again, one doesn't want a flat picture. And a picture can be given depth by suitable lighting.' 'Suitable lighting' involved the use of numerous lamps and of course this generates heat. Peter Byrne points out the potential dangers: 'Back in 1953 it must have been like the early days of Hollywood. There were no techniques to relate it to. We were still using the old-fashioned film lighting – huge floods – and the intensity of the heat was dreadful, particularly if you were on at nine o'clock at night and you had come in at ten o'clock in the morning. With the advent of colour, when you left the set they could bring the lights down and it was much cooler in the studio. In those days they would have to leave the lights on all day because it took quite a long time for them to warm up. You could always tell somebody who had been in television before 1960 because they had a pitted face down one side [i.e. nicked by splinters of glass from exploding lights]. On occasions these lights would overheat and during live transmissions you would be standing very close to this huge flood and it would explode. The actor who didn't blink was the one who had been in television before 1960 – you learned to control yourself.'

James Grout shares similar memories: 'There was always a certain amount of light spilling from the sets, but not a lot. If one set was lit in the corner of the studio, the rest of the studio would be fairly murky. High up in the corner of the studio was one tiny little fan, two feet wide at the most, so it used to get exceedingly warm. The lighting was nothing like as sophisticated as it is now, it was very powerful and you had a lot of wattage thrown down on you.' Judy Campbell recalls the solution: 'We had people running after us with chamois leather dipped in eau-de-Cologne because it was terribly, terribly hot. Coca-Cola had just been invented and I remember having drinks of Coca-Cola to cool us down.'

Roy Glew, who worked as an engineer, offers insight into some of the other duties of the Lighting Department, namely to create special effects, although some of the methods that were employed seem crude if not downright dangerous by modern standards. 'One of the things we never had in a satisfactory form was a lightning-effects unit. If you wanted to reproduce the effects of lightning it was very difficult. In the old days they would get an electrician, put a welding mask with a colour visor on his head and make him wear rubber gloves. In one hand he would hold a big metal file that was attached to a very good earth by a very thick copper wire and in the other hand he would hold a carbon rod that was attached to a 450-volt DC supply that they used for the carbon lamps. He would strike the carbon rod against the metal file, which of course produced a terrific flash. Once you've actually struck the file and got your initial contact and produced a flash, you could then maintain a little arc for a few seconds. Health and Safety would never stand for it now. It required a very brave electrician to do all this.' Glew also explains how another, less hazardous effect was achieved. 'To get the effect of flickering firelight we used to have an electrician holding a piece of stick with some bunting strips attached to it, which he would waft backwards and forwards in front of a lamp.'

As part of his general work experience, Roy Glew also

did his time on sound, operating the boom to which the microphone was attached. 'I worked on the series called the *Honeyman Lectures*. There were fifteen or so paintings around three walls of the set and Dr Honeyman would move around, talking about the artistic merits of each. He always ended the programme sitting in a very deep arm-chair and I was then working as a boom operator. I was tracked in to lower the boom to about eighteen inches above his forehead and the camera was tracked in for a head-and-shoulders close-up. He started his summary and after about thirty seconds he suddenly said, "Let's go back to picture number seven"! And without any more ado he bounded up out of the armchair. There was a terrific crash as his head hit my boom microphone – they were great big microphones in those days – and he slowly slipped back into his chair unconscious. We had to fade sound and vision, and that was the end of that programme.'

Creating sound effects could be almost as much of a headache. 'I remember working in the studio at Springfield Road in Glasgow,' says Glew, 'and we needed to put some reverberation, an echo, on one of our sound channels. There was a technical machine for doing this but it had broken down, so for some reason we decided to put a microphone in the gents in order to get the echo. Of course, right at the critical moment during the live trans-mission, the toilet flushed, so not only did we get the rever-beration, we got the sound of a flushing loo as well.'

One particular special effect that many actors appear to recollect with mixed emotions was the use of back projec-tion. This was a means of making stationary cars appear to be travelling at speed, and Leonard Lewis describes how it was done. 'In *Z Cars* all the scenes inside cars were shot in a truncated version of the Ford Zephyr, with back projection that was either moving or still. The back projection was sent a great distance through mirrors. It wasn't a simple small space in the studio; the whole length of the studio was used for back projection, which meant that nobody must walk across it.' George Cole reveals that even this crude form of technology was not failsafe: 'In order to give the impression that a car was moving at speed they used "back projection". On one occasion the BP got stuck and the car appeared to be travelling at speed when it was supposed to stop. One actor turned to the other and said, "You'd better go round the block again." Having done that, the BP was still running and the actor had to open the car door and say, "I'd better jump out," which he did.' This poor unfortunate could well have been Colin Welland: 'I had to jump out of a car going at sixty miles per hour because the back projection got stuck.'

A key member of the studio staff, who often liaised between the various departments and did a good deal of legwork in the process, was the assistant floor manager. David London began his career in this way. 'I started off as an assistant floor manager, they called them floor assistants in those days. Basically you had to do the running about, the fetching, putting up captions for the end credits. It was a lot of running round, getting people out of the loo – "Come on, you're on stage now!"' Leonard Lewis describes his duties as AFM during the rehearsal period. 'Often you had to move the furniture as the run was going on, while watching the book and keeping the director happy with a cup of tea. The other thing you did as an AFM was to make up a list of the props; you sort of helped to run the rehearsals.' Things did not become any simpler once the show reached the studio: 'As an assistant floor manager you were on the book, you prompted. On transmission you had the cut key in your hand and you travelled around the studio and if an actor dried you cut the sound from the studio and then shouted out the prompt. The AFM did all the dogsbody jobs. I remember once an actor was ill and unable to appear and someone else was brought in at the last moment. The poor AFM, which was me, had to read his part in during the day while he was trying to learn it and they were preparing it on autocue for that night.' (The presenter Keith Martin is able to provide insight into what it was like to operate the autocue machine: 'I used to get the equipment working for people on *Nationwide, Panorama, Take your Pick* – all of them used the autocue. Each camera had rolls of paper underneath and you actually typed every word on each piece of paper in enormous letter faces. Unfortunately from time to time it used to tear, then they would cut to the other camera, desperately hoping that one wouldn't tear as well.')

Margaret Tabor worked as a stage manager in the days of live television and paints a vivid picture of what this could entail. 'I had to crouch underneath the lens of the camera in order to hand actors props, remove props, and sometimes start removing their clothes ready for a quick change – often the actor would be doing a very poignant speech while this was going on.' On another occasion a scene had been cut because the play had overrun, and she remembers giving the cue and the actor hissing back, 'The scene's cut, the scene's cut!' She gave the cue again and the actor refused to do it and in the end he was proved to be right. The terrifying tension of live television made mistakes more likely, as Bernard Hepton reveals: 'In the early days when things went out live people's nerves were of the highest degree, strung like a violin. One studio manager was particularly known for getting himself in a stew and he was once observed actually cueing the wall.'

The studio or floor manager provided a vital link between the director and the cast. 'We seemed to have quite a reasonable amount of rehearsal time in those days, when you got to know the director terribly well and your fellow-actors. When you came to do it the director disappeared into his little box, and you relied on the floor manager,' Stephen Hancock explains. 'They were absolutely superb, they were rocks, and they guided you through the whole dreadful business.' David London outlines his responsibilities. 'The role of the floor manager on the studio floor is to be the eyes and ears of the director. You're on the floor, you have your headphones on and your script. You are there to make sure that the artists are in the right place, holding the right thing, and that they get cued when the little red light on the camera comes on.'

A huge amount of work was put in during the run-up to transmission by those concerned with how a programme would look. In particular, designers at Alexandra Palace took time and trouble to evolve the kind of scenery that would photograph well on television. In an early edition of the *Radio Times*, Peter Bax talks of 'our search for an effective compromise between the three-dimensional architecture of the cinema studio and the flat painted scenery of the stage', and goes on to say:

> Scenery, like everything else connected with the new and start-
> ling art of television, has had to be approached from the
> humble position of tentative experiment. We began at
> Alexandra Palace with curtains. These afforded the best starting
> point as they were convenient for all sorts of programmes and
> could be worked in well with more elaborate scenery later. For
> about a month, therefore, our backgrounds consisted of black or
> white curtains or a combination of both. During this period we
> in the production department learnt a good deal about studio
> conditions, and particularly what our cameras liked and dis-
> liked, and it appeared that a more neutral-tinted setting was ne-
> cessary. After a few trials (and errors) we decided on some tones
> of pale grey and several 'flats' were made and carefully painted.

The actor Paul Williamson recalls that these flats were not terribly robust: 'The sets were pretty flimsy, so you had to be careful not to slam the door or all the pictures on the wall shook.' Leonard Lewis observes that 'The sets were brought into the studio and joined together and the paint-ers and the carpenters would be around doing the repairs. Because it was in black and white the detail didn't show so badly and you got away with things, but you couldn't put those sets up today. All the faults would show up now; with digital you get even more detail and it becomes more diffi-cult. That's one of the reasons that now you work less and less in studio and more and more on location.'

Bax goes on to reveal that not only was the Design Department responsible for the sets, they were also concerned with making or finding the necessary props. '"Properties", all the various furnishings and details which augment the scenery, have also to be constructed. Our producers have, apparently, limitless imaginations and we must therefore be prepared to construct the most incongruous mass of articles. Thus a morning's work might consist of supplying a volcano, a ghost, a harpsichord and a couple of cacti.'

Sometimes the designer's artistic vision could be compromised when the time came for transmission, recalls Barbara Lott: 'I remember playing Viola in a live production of *Twelfth Night*; it must have been one of the first Shakespeares done on television. The designer had the idea that we'd have plastic screens placed at angles to each other and they would back-project beautiful Elizabethan rooms and Elizabethan gardens, and it would all look wonderful. During the live transmission the back projection broke down, so it just looked as if we were performing in a bathroom.'

The provision of costumes also seems to have been something of a hit-and-miss affair. Eileen Atkins remembers playing Joan of Arc in *Age of Kings*. 'They didn't make their own costumes then [1960], so they hired Jean Seberg's armour for me. She was only five foot two and I am five foot seven. It was so uncomfortable.' Margaret Tyzack recounts another occasion when an actor was afflicted with ill-fitting clothes. 'I remember doing a show for ABC in the Didsbury studios in Manchester. The leading man appeared looking as though he was wearing lederhosen because his trousers had been shrunk by Wardrobe in the wash.' Peggy Mount described a colleague being reduced to tears by the frock provided for her. 'I remember that Lally Bowers made a guest appearance in an episode of *The Larkins*. She had to be very smart; she wore old-fashioned clothes, but smart. Lally Bowers came on to the set in tears . . . She was saying, "Peggy, I can't wear this, can I?" I looked, and of course she couldn't. It had been made specially for her, with the skirt and the peplum of the time. I said, "We'll find you something else, Lally, don't you worry." "Well, I can't wear this," Lally said, and she sat down but the dress stayed up. She looked just like a tortoise, it was the funniest thing I've ever seen.'

To be fair to the Wardrobe Department, shooting programmes in black and white made great demands upon their talents. Ian Flintoff explains: '*Emergency Ward 10* was shot in black and white and when I got into the studio I was astonished to see that all the doctors' and nurses' uniforms and their hats were all yellow. They were almost amber-coloured. If they had been white, there would have been a considerable flare from the cruder forms of studio lighting.'

Leslie Lawton explains another consequence of the harsh lighting. 'The lighting was fairly primitive. They used bright white light that tended to wash things out, which is why make-up was used to put your features back in.' Accounts vary as to which shade was favoured. John Warner remembered, 'I played at Alexandra Palace in the old days, it was very primitive and you had this extraordinary make-up which you wore for black and white television, it was sort of yellow.' However, James Grout's recollection is that, 'It was a kind of pale green. I think it had something to do with the tones needed for black and white.' Mary Allen, who was the principal make-up artist at Alexandra Palace, set the record straight in an interview for an early edition of the *Radio Times*.

My usual procedure is to watch the screen during the rehearsals, and I find it very necessary to attend these, for I am able to compare notes with the engineers and watch the balance of light and shade, which is of great importance in making a first-class picture . . . In the film studios definite basic colours are applied, requiring perhaps only alterations of shades in colour for blondes and brunettes, besides the necessary shading on the cheeks and eyes. Usually the cameraman will discuss with the makeup expert the shade he prefers, in order to get the desired effect. From my experiments during the last six months I have found it practically impossible to follow the same principle for television. In the first place, the viewing screen being still small, everything must be worked out on a smaller scale . . . Today a makeup of grey or peach colour foundation may seem to be an ideal shade, tomorrow owing to a lighting problem or a change of costume, the same colour proves to be entirely wrong . . . it may be of interest, however, to know that we no longer use blue on lips and eyes. Many artists come here expecting to use bright green on the lips. This idea is entirely without foundation for that colour has never been used. An ordinary red lipstick is perfectly satisfactory . . . Generally speaking, we have found it wise to avoid black or dark-coloured materials, the most effective shades being yellow, pale blue, pink, mauve and beige, all these colours help extensively in dressing a scene where a good deal of light is required.

Janet Hargreaves recalls that the overall effect could look bizarre. 'Because it was black and white the make-up was very heavy; they literally sculpted your face. I used to have white circles painted round my eyes so that the bags under them wouldn't show. It looked horrendous, I was only twenty-three! There were far more limitations over what you could wear with black and white television – you couldn't wear anything black and white or checked or striped because the picture strobed.' Margaret Tyzack's recollection is equally rueful: 'I looked as though my face had been dipped in a flour barrel because the make-up was very different then.'

George Baker found that revealing some of the tricks of the make-up department was not always advisable. 'My make-up for *I, Claudius*, when I was playing Tiberius as a very old, very nasty old man, started at four in the morning and took eleven hours. I had to have a bald head first. For my skin we used cornflakes. We were having breakfast one morning and the make-up artist was having cornflakes and I said, "My God, that looks like a wonderful scab!" So we glued it on and she painted it and it did make a wonderful scab. I was asked to do a talk for the people at Kellogg's in Manchester and I thought that would be a frightfully good thing to tell them. I cannot tell you what a stony silence there was. The fact that their product was used for a syphilitic scab did not go down well!'

Other trade secrets are revealed by Josephine Tewson. 'My first live television was with Ben Lyon and Bebe Daniels. I remember I was in the make-up room under the hairdrier and they both came in for their make-up. Ben Lyon just took what looked like boot polish and a brush and brushed in the crown of his head where he was bald. That was it; he went out. Bebe Daniels had her hair put up in pin curls and then had some very, very, very fine black gauze stretched under her chin and pinned behind her ears, which took any jowls out. She also had paperclips under her hair, pulling her eyes back. It was a kind of temporary facelift. Then she had the make-up done and the wig put on top of all of this. She looked about forty-five at the end of all of this and she must have been God knows how old. When it came to my turn the make-up artist looked at me and said, "What's your name?" And I said, "Josephine Tewson." And she looked down the cast list, where they'd obviously written what was wanted for make-up, and said, "Ah, yes." She then went off to get something. Stupidly I leaned over to see what was written against my name. I thought it might say, "Rouge on the cheeks" and it said, "Remedial". I thought, *That'll teach you!*'

All actors can be vulnerable creatures in the make-up room, a point endorsed by Michael Kilgarriff. 'I once had to play a character who was very tall and very handsome and I had to wear a long blond wig. I really looked quite whizzo! I remember on one occasion going to make-up and the girl put the wig on and said, "You look just like Roberta Cowell!" I was not pleased. Roberta Cowell was the first publicized sex change. I said, "Well, thank you very much, that's very nice!"' Mary Kenton offers some sympathy: 'One looked so horrendous on television in those days, because all the lighting was top-lighting. You needed to be young and pretty healthy to look good. I remember Robert Flemyng seeing himself on the monitor one day during a camera rehearsal and he said, "Oh God, and I used to be so beautiful!"'

With so many different skills being required to nurture a show to the point of transmission, and so many different arts and trades called upon, it is unsurprising to discover that the unions were a powerful force in live television. Bob Holness throws light on just how much muscle they had. 'The crews were wonderful in those days; they were regularly employed by the television companies. I don't ever remember seeing freelance sound operators, or freelance graphics people. They had assured jobs and a very heavy union. The union was absolutely implacable in its demands to the management. I remember one little incident which I will never forget; it was when the Pilkington report on radio and television came out. We were doing *What the Papers Say* and you read the excerpts from the screen as they came up. I sat there with the other presenter, Brian Trueman, and we went through a rehearsal and I said to Brian, "There's a box of broken glass down here on the floor next to me." He explained that he would announce the report and instead of a little fanfare they would have the sound of breaking glass. I thought that was rather ingenious. We got to the last rehearsal before we went on air and there was no one around and I bent down and just rattled this broken glass in the box and the entire studio came to a halt. There was a circle of cameras around us and all the cameramen stopped, stood by their cameras and folded their arms. Jeremy Isaacs, who was the producer, came running down the stairs from the control room in the gallery and said, "What the Dickens did you do that for?" I said, "There was no one about," and he said, "There will be when we transmit. You're not supposed to touch that; it's not your job; your job is to talk. You don't rattle boxes of glass, that's up to the props man, he has to do that." He had to go round to every one of the cameramen and explain that I was a new guy, that I didn't know the rules and that honestly I wouldn't do it again. They relented in the end, but they were governed by their rules.'

Some actors thought that their own union, Equity, would have done well to be as robust as its sister body the National Association of Theatrical, Television and Kine Engineers. Michael Kilgarriff comments, 'The studios used to get terribly hot . . . If it got too hot there were regulations for NATKE – not actors, but NATKE members wouldn't work if it got too hot so all the lights were cut out to cool the studio down.'

8

On the Receiving End

THE WORKING ETHOS at the BBC in the earliest days was articulated in the first royal charter granted to it in 1927, which stipulated that the Corporation should inform, educate and entertain its audience, while maintaining political and editorial independence. These lofty ambitions were to be the cornerstone of what was to become known as public-service broadcasting, where the emphasis was placed firmly on satisfying the perceived needs (as opposed to desires) of the viewer. The actors who were involved in live television describe the choice of programmes on offer in tones that are generally admiring. Malcolm Farquhar gives a rough description of the kind of fare that was available on post-war television: 'In the late forties there was only one channel and a whole evening's entertainment was *What's My Line?* and a play.'

His fleeting reference to 'a play' does not really do justice to the quality of the drama that, according to George Baker, was soon to be available. 'In the late fifties we were just beginning to go into the era of really wonderful television – *Armchair Theatre*, *The Wednesday Play*, *Play of the*

Month. I was very lucky to be part of that.' Richard O'Callaghan mourns the passing of this period. 'I think that television, certainly on the drama side, has collapsed. There was a time when you had *Play for Today*, *Armchair Theatre*, *The Wednesday Play*, the *Play of the Month*. We were fed two or three plays a week of an incredibly high calibre.' And it was not just the public-service BBC who provided quality drama. 'The great thing about working for the BBC was that they concentrated very strongly on doing the classics, wonderful Dickens serials and things like that,' remarks Trevor Bannister. 'The cost of everything in those days was very much less, salaries were less, everything was less and therefore productions were much larger and much more ambitious. Independent television, when it began to grow, began to do some wonderful plays – The *Armchair Theatre*s and the *Midweek Theatre*s.' George Baker also bears witness to the high quality of work on the commercial channel. 'Sydney Newman insisted on new plays and new writers for *Armchair Theatre* and people really were trying to stretch the medium as far as it could go and see what they could do with it. It was an incredible time. Jack Rosenthal was producing *Coronation Street* and writing for it. People like Tony Garnett, Kenith Trodd, the marvellous thing about them was their vision for television.'

Like Richard O'Callaghan, Trevor Bannister thinks that the schedules today suffer by comparison to the ones of fifty years ago. 'There was an awful lot of drama and serials, we weren't filled up with quiz shows and gardening and cookery programmes and police-chases-down-motorways programmes.' Recalling his work as a presenter in the 1960s, David Hamilton notes that 'In those days ATV had a very strong schedule for Sunday night. There was *The Avengers* followed by *Sunday Night at the London Palladium*, followed by *Armchair Theatre*, followed by *The Maverick*. It was such a strong schedule that everybody went to work on Monday morning talking about the same television programmes. It would never happen now.'

Extraordinarily ambitious projects were embarked upon. In November 1962 ITV took an astonishing decision for a channel solely dependent on commercial funding when it transmitted Sophocles' *Electra* in the original Greek – it would be a brave producer who would attempt a similar undertaking in the twenty-first century. The BBC was also 'earnest in many ways, but it was honest and it had a great integrity', according to Nigel Hawthorne. Possibly the most famous example of this type of broadcasting was Ken Loach's *Cathy Come Home*, which exposed the problem of homelessness in Britain. The impact of this play (by Jeremy Sandford) was so intense that it prompted the government to review its housing policy and also led to the foundation of the charity Shelter.

Not all of the output was as close to the cutting edge as *Cathy Come Home*, but many programmes had worthy intentions and closely followed the charter's exhortation to inform and educate. Peter Byrne was involved in a particularly high-minded project. 'Ted Willis wrote a dramatized documentary called *The Pattern of Marriage*. The dramatized documentaries in those days were wonderful. The war had been over for a few years, we were coming to the end of rationing, there was a tremendous housing shortage, national service was in so young men just kicked their heels between the ages of sixteen and eighteen. The country was virtually on its knees and bankrupt. There was a hell of a lot of emigration . . . There were a lot of social issues to be dealt with. It was terribly difficult to get a divorce, but forty thousand marriages were breaking down each year. They put all the problems of these forty thousand marriages on to Billie [Whitelaw] and me. It dealt with ordinary people, it didn't have heavy political overtones. They were very powerful pieces.'

Byrne also points out that there was an ethical undertone to even the most popular fare: 'There was a strong moral content in *Dixon of Dock Green* but it reflected the times. Police work is really terribly boring; a lot of it is luck. Policemen are a lot jollier than they are presented – there's a lot of laughter, they drink a lot of tea and there's a lot of black humour – but they have a diabolical life. Ted Willis broke new ground because he showed that they were ordinary men doing an extraordinary job. They had families and by the nature of the job their families were somehow set aside from the community. Previously they'd been portrayed by Agatha Christie as rather stupid country yokels. Ours led the way and spawned *Z Cars*, *Softly Softly* and *The Sweeney*.' Eve Pearce says that the research underpinning *Z Cars* was meticulous: '*Z Cars* was enormously well set up. Originally a producer called Gilchrist Calder and a writer called Colin Morris had done some famous documentaries; it was quite a new idea in those days. From that somebody had the idea of doing the same kind of thing with the police. They would really, really research it, not just on the surface. They got hold of a man who had just retired from the Liverpool force, he was famous for getting confessions out of criminals, he was a psychological wizard, and he knew when to go in, when to lay off, when to sympathize. He had a fund of stories, a fund of actual cases, and all the writers were told to go and talk to him. He helped them formulate what the various characters would be like. It meant that they were very clear who these people were and what they did. It was extremely well cast. It had a lot of wonderful writers – John Hopkins wrote a great number of them himself; he then became the editor as well and he was extremely helpful to the writers.'

According to Stephen Hancock, even medical soaps such as *Emergency Ward 10* were used as vehicles for public information. 'I played a character called Dr Faulkner. He had a wife who was pregnant and suddenly got polio and spent all her time in an iron lung. It was a teaching thing really, to reassure the watching public that you could have polio and survive and give birth successfully to a baby. Most of the stories were like that, they featured something which might happen to you to show people that it wasn't the end of the world. It was educational, it was a public service and entertainment at the same time.'

Hilary Mason was involved in a play that could be seen as a precursor to the 'reality TV' so popular with today's audiences. '*England, This England* was a series in six episodes designed to help people who were in difficulties. One was about a pregnant girl, it showed what she could do, where she could go. Mine was about a woman whose husband had emphysema. This poor woman had given up her job. They were not allowed to use the real person so I was going to play her, but everybody else, and it was the same in all the series, was played by real people. You had no script at all, you had to make it up as you went along. They treated you as if you were the real person; I went to meet her, I met the husband too. The whole thing was terrifying, you never knew what they were going to ask you to do. They sent me along to the electricity board because the woman couldn't pay her electricity bill. They said it could be paid weekly.' Miriam Karlin provides an example of the effect that these kinds of issue-based programmes could have, as she played Paddy, the shop steward in the comedy series *The Rag Trade*. 'In the last few years I've been a delegate from Equity to the TUC and I've taken enormous pleasure in the number of women who've said, "We got interested in trade unions because of you." I was really knocked out, really excited – they regarded me as a sort of role model. It never occurred to me that I was doing any good.'

Both the BBC and ITV took their broadcasting responsibilities seriously. Not only did they strive to offer an informative as well as an entertaining service for the nation, they held high standards with regard to the kind of material to which the public may or may not be exposed. (This restraint applied to the wireless as much as it did to television. Maurice Denham recalls, '*Much Binding in the Marsh* was the cleanest radio ever, I think. Not that it had been dirty before. *Round the Horne* was more humorous, more outspoken. There was a whole list of things you couldn't say, particularly on radio. You couldn't say "knickers". You couldn't say, "Oh Lord." You have to respect the most susceptible and the others have to suffer.') Dallas Bower maintains that this protectiveness was not the result of external pressure. 'There was no censorship in the BBC except the Corporation's self-imposed censorship,' but Edward Jewesbury reveals that occasionally the censorship did originate from outside. 'David Turner wrote a play about local government called *Swizzlewick* and we filmed it in Birmingham. It was done in Restoration style and all of the characters had names like Mr Chiseller. It was a great send-up of local government, and the city council got to hear about it. They insisted on seeing all the scripts before we did it. It got to a stage where they would come down – we were about to do it live that evening – and they would say, "You can't say that, you must have another line put in there," and David Turner got so fed up with it that he refused to write any more and other people took over, but it was never the same.'

Hilary Mason is another veteran of *Swizzlewick*. 'It was all about town councils and corruption, and people used to write in from all over England – "Our town council isn't anything like this!" We got lots of letters, some furious letters. I played a Birmingham landlady who had a lodger, played by a lovely actor called Haydn Jones. His character used to have a bath in front of the fire. It was a tin bath because there was no proper bathroom. I used to have a kettle and fill it up with hot water. I knocked on the door while Haydn was getting undressed. He put a towel round his middle and the towel slipped on camera and showed his navel. The programme went out live at half-past six. For the very first time Mrs Whitehouse was on to the studio within about ten minutes – "You can't do this! There are children watching this!"'

Mary Whitehouse was the vociferous founder of the National Viewers' and Listeners' Association, which she launched in 1965. She saw herself as a defender of the country's morals, and both television channels were cautious about what they broadcast in order to avoid provoking the kind of reaction for which she was famous. Maria Charles maintains that they could not always predict what the level of audience response would be: 'I was in *The Voice of the Turtle* at Lime Grove, directed by Stuart Burge . . . Elvi [Hale] was seen in her slip and there was a great fuss made about that afterwards. People were saying that it was disgusting and disgraceful and it shouldn't be put on. We knew it was a bit bold, but we didn't expect that kind of reaction.'

According to Harry Landis, not everybody was willing to compromise. 'I did a thing called *Crane* with Patrick Allen. The show went out at 7 p.m. and it all took place in some Arab land with villains wearing fezzes. Laya Raki was in it. She was half German, half Javanese, and had an exotic Oriental look, and she played a *femme fatale*. One day they called her in and said, "I'm afraid there have been complaints. People have rung up and said your bosom is too low." Wardrobe was given strict instructions to check her costume before transmission and sew it up. She wanted it to be revealing. She was standing next to me and we were waiting to go on and she ripped the stitching apart and went straight on. I thought that was wonderful; that took a lot of bottle.'

From the earliest days, the BBC was keen to monitor public opinion of its work. In the very first issue of the *Radio Times Television Supplement* they published an article, 'News For You Viewers – Viewers to Join Up', which issued the following invitation: 'In the television transmission on Boxing Day a preliminary announcement was made asking viewers to send their names and addresses on a postcard to the BBC, who will then write to them period-

ically to ask various questions about reception and programmes . . . it is felt that invaluable help in this pioneer
stage of television service can be given if viewers will give
comments and criticism.' Two years later, in June 1939, the
approach was hardly more sophisticated – a group of
viewers was invited to a tea party in the concert hall at
Broadcasting House to discuss their responses to programming.

The BBC assessed the success of its earliest attempts at
market research in an internal memo:

> From its first inception the television service has made a point of
> encouraging viewers to write in, giving their reactions to any
> programme item on which they might desire to express an
> opinion . . . With the great increase of viewers during the year
> 1938 it was decided that a more definite census of viewers' opin-
> ions should be taken and, accordingly, a questionnaire was
> drawn up for circulation to viewers . . . The response was highly
> gratifying and a seventy five percent return was received. The
> questionnaire consisted of thirteen questions, many of them
> sub-divided into two or three parts. The result of the analysis of
> these returns proved to be extraordinarily close to the informa-
> tion derived from casual comment of viewers received prior to
> the issue of the questionnaire and showed that plays, news reels,
> light entertainment and *Picture Page* (television's topical weekly
> magazine) were the most popular items, with outside events,
> films and demonstrations following in their percentage of votes.
> There was an overwhelming majority in favour of women
> announcers as opposed to men, the result being exactly opposite
> to that of sound's questionnaire on the same subject. Opinion
> was very evenly divided on the question of the length of pro-
> grammes. Another interesting point was that the average
> number of people viewing each set was four, this giving a poten-
> tial audience of sixty thousand people per transmission. This

number is increasing very rapidly. The policy of gaining individual opinion and close contact between service and viewers is being maintained and is held to be of the greatest value. From time to time methods other than the questionnaire will be adopted so as to obtain opinions on points affecting transmission hours etc.

Dick Sharples describes how this process eventually evolved into what was known as the Audience Appreciation Index. 'People used to go from door to door saying, "How did you rate such and such a show in terms of satisfaction?" The Audience Appreciation Index used to be more important to the BBC than the ratings, because they weren't going after numbers then. If a programme had a minority audience but people were saying, "Great show!" it stayed on. That's how it used to be, it's not now.'

Just as the public was quick to contact the broadcasters if they disapproved of what was transmitted, they were also keen to enter into all kinds of direct dialogue with the performers themselves. Trevor Bannister remarks, 'Some members of the public have a feeling that you belong to them and that you are only appearing in their house and not in the one next door. People respond to you in a very personalized way; they use your Christian name even though you've never met them before.' The presenter Adrian Cairns also highlights the significance of appearing in the home of the viewers. 'When you do that sort of thing [presenting on Tyne Tees], you're accepted across the whole structure of society because you've been in their room, in a funny kind of way. There you are in the corner of their sitting room and you're a friend of the family.'

David Hamilton reveals how on occasions this illusion of

intimacy was deliberately cultivated. 'When we finished at the end of the evening I developed a tag line, "A special good-night to you," because I wanted to personalize it. People, particularly women, used to write to me and say, "I liked it when you said good-night because I knew you were saying it just to me." I think it was a great shame when the television companies, probably for economic reasons, took the announcers out of vision. Until then, we were viewed as a friend in the home. It was as though there was some-body at the station watching the programmes with you. That got you a kind of station loyalty.' Ian Flintoff points out that this kind of virtual friendship could be strong: 'My son was actually born while I was on air and Kenneth Kendall who was doing the links on the programme announced the news on air live and we were sent all sorts of little knitted jackets, which was very kind. I never had any hate mail of any kind. I was asked to kick off football matches and judge local beauty competitions as a sort of PR exercise.'

According to Shaw Taylor, members of the public were sometimes perplexed by the vague familiarity that they sensed. 'Once I drove into a garage for some petrol. The attendant said the usual "I have met you before, haven't I?" I said no but he wasn't convinced. "Were you in the RAF?" he asked. I said I was and we went through the camps we had been stationed at but none coincided. Then we went through our life stories, without success. But when I'd got back in the car and he saw me through the screen-shaped windowframe he exclaimed, "Of course, you're on television!"'

Because members of the television audience felt that

they were on familiar terms with the actors they watched, they were not backward in voicing any opinions about their work. Peter Bowles remembers, 'Everybody used to talk about what they'd seen on television, that's what they used to talk about every day, so if you'd been in a play they'd be talking about you. If you went into a shop, the chances are that everyone in the shop would have seen you on television. You certainly found out what they felt about it. Because you'd been in their front room the night before they felt they could say, "Saw you in the show last night, didn't like it." It was very refreshing. If you act in a film and you're walking down the street, people will nudge each other and whisper, "Look, that's So-and-so." If you work on television it'll be, "Oy! Pete! 'Allo! How are you?!"'

Colin Welland is another who relished this kind of contact. 'The immediacy was marvellous. You'd go up to the bar after and get an immediate response from people there, and the next day the butcher or the binman would say, "Saw you last night. . . ."' Eve Pearce however experienced the rough end of public criticism: 'I did two of the original *Dr Finlay's Casebook*s. In one of them I played an older part; I was much too young for it. The next day a couple passed me in the street and the woman looked at me and said, "I said at the time she was much too young for it and she is!"'

What these anecdotes reveal is how literally some viewers respond to what they see on the box. Hilary Mason describes the extremes of this: 'When I was in *United*, which was about a football team, in one episode the manager was sacked and somebody wrote in to the programme stating their qualifications and asking if they could have his job! People did take television very literally.'

(And they still do. Although it is decades since Peter Byrne last appeared in *Dixon of Dock Green*, the illusion created by the show lingers on. 'You were in their homes, it was the miracle of the age and if they actually saw you they went berserk. They'd tear your clothes off. Even to this day people still call me Mr Crawford and ask how Mary and the twins are.') Leslie Lawton had a similar experience. 'In an early episode of *Coronation Street* my girlfriend was having an affair with Ken Barlow, and I remember walking from the station down to Granada and this taxi driver screeched to a halt, wound down his window and said, "Listen, I think you should know . . ." In 1963 you didn't have the phrase "Get a life!" '

To many actors this kind of experience brought home the huge influence of the broadcast media. Miriam Karlin says, 'Being in *The Rag Trade* was the first time that I realized the power of television. Cab drivers in particular used to say things like, "I come from your part, you know." And I'd say, "Where is that, then?" They'd say, "The East End," and I'd say, "I'm sorry, I don't know it at all." Then I'd feel dreadfully embarrassed at having to say I was born in Hampstead.' Stephen Hancock comments, 'My first telly was in 1953. I didn't realize at the time the enormous power of this television thing. There were not many sets around in those days, but I remember after the first transmission I did, which was a sitcom called *Dear Dottie* with Avril Angers, that I was waiting for a bus and the driver drew up, slid back his window and said, "How's Dottie?" Even then, you didn't realize the power of the thing, you didn't realize what would be happening in twenty years' time, when all you had to do was to appear on television and you became a star.'

George Baker describes the downside to this public exposure and adulation. 'This man wrote to me and said that his wife was sleeping with my picture under her pillow and could we possibly meet and he would be delighted to buy me dinner, because it was tormenting him. I wrote back and said that I was awfully sorry, and so on. I didn't think that I could get involved in that. I didn't think that would be wise. But it showed you the terrific power of television.'

Over the years this credulousness has evolved into a kind of prurience. It is not enough for the viewers to treat the actors and the situations that they witness as though they were real, as they tended to do at the outset; the current trend in ratings reveals an appetite for programmes in which the participants *are* real people. This has given rise to a new genre of programme, the so-called docu-soap or 'reality TV', which charts the progress of ordinary members of the public as they learn to drive, train as vets, or work on cruise liners, in airports or hotels. Culminating in the definitive model of this kind of entertainment, *Big Brother*, it is a form of entertainment that reflects our own lives back to us. Just as the national lottery holds out the flickering allure of fabulous wealth, so reality TV suggests to the average person that almost anyone has a chance of celebrity. In a sense it provides affirmation of every individual's potential and at the same time appeals to the voyeuristic side of people's natures. This is a potent combination that television producers have been eager to exploit, not least because using non-professionals is cheaper than hiring actors.

Reality TV can be seen as the logical outcome of television's attempt to find its unique form, something that sets it apart from the theatre and film. Adrian Cairns believes that 'Drama is a shadow of life and today it has to be true shadow. In the past you could get away with tatty sets. Now you see the "real" thing, so real that people take it to be the real thing.' Margaret Tyzack highlights the fact that it was in the area of design that the move towards realism first became apparent. 'The biggest difference between television now and television then is that now so much is shot on location and in those days it was all done in studio.' Just as the setting of plays became more realistic – even 'real' – so, Brian Murphy thinks, casting became more accurate. 'Actors used to be allowed to do performances and the audience accepted it; now you are totally typecast.'

Peter Byrne suggests that the trend towards 'reality' was anticipated as early as the 1950s, when practitioners were speculating about the future course of the fledgeling medium. 'Kenneth Adam, who used to be the Director of Television, said a very significant thing to me once: "The pure television is the outside broadcast, it's the immediacy of something happening now." I think it's true that drama really hasn't found its place in television. Pure television is going out into the street and sticking a microphone under somebody's nose when something ghastly is happening, or just talking to an ordinary person, or recording an exciting event.' In Brian Murphy's opinion, this process of self-identification is continuous. 'I don't think the nature of television has yet been truly discovered. I think they're still picking at it. It borrowed heavily in its initial history from the theatre and in later years from the cinema. Its actual nature, as it were, I don't think has yet been purified. It's something straightforward and direct to us.'

One of the stranger effects of this shift towards reality in television is that, just as drama and entertainment become 'real', so real events themselves become more filmic. The horrific events of 11 September 2001 were beamed around the world as they unfolded, and the millions watching the carnage take place on their screens at home in the manner of some disaster movie must have entertained the brief, surreal hope that the hero would come striding on to the scene and put everything right. The narrative of those events had an epic quality that transcended actuality.

The dynamics of the relationship between television and its audience have changed enormously. The Reithian ideal to serve the public by educating as well as entertaining them has been hijacked by the competitiveness between the various channels, which is articulated in the weekly publication of the programme ratings. Brian Murphy comments, 'I know competition is healthy, but in television it has got to an almost war-like level. There is a battle between the channels to grab the audience. People used to want to make programmes and to make them as well as they could, which seems to me a good intent, but now the motive seems to be to grab attention from the opposition and in that way you start to lose the name of the game.' Nigel Hawthorne endorsed this point of view: 'Today television companies are too much impressed by viewing figures. I never really believed that the BBC had anything to do with viewing figures – the public pays their licence fee and therefore they should be going for quality, rather than quantity of audience. If we don't maintain that quality we will become like American movies, where you can't make a film because they say, "Well, who's it for?"

If it's not expected to make a lot of money, they won't make it. It's tragic, isn't it?' Hawthorne was not the only person to see parallels with the American system. Edward Jewesbury declares that 'If we go like America, when they have fifty channels, it can only get worse. Originally we only had one BBC channel and the quality of it was terrific. Then commercial television came along and that was good because it generated competition, but now . . .!' As Leslie Lawton says, 'What's the point of having forty-odd channels? Can't we go back to having two good ones?' Brian Murphy thinks that broadcasting output is becoming too thinly spread. 'There are so many hours now to fill, with the competition from cable and satellite, but we're still only a potential audience of about fifty million and you begin to wonder how much can we see. There is so much of it now that we are exposed to much more inferior stuff than we used to be.'

The tyranny of the ratings means not only that programming for minority interests is in danger of being squeezed, but also that Reith's ethic of playing to the strengths of the audience rather than pandering to their weaknesses is under threat. Bernard Hepton laments, 'I have heard over and over again in radio and television, the people in the offices with carpets up to their knees saying, "We must give the public what they want." I can tell them that the public does not know what they want. It is a totally wrong assumption. What must happen, and what used to happen, was that the public were given what the person in charge thought was right and hoped they would like. And nearly always they did like it. In those days nobody said, "What would the public like?" They said, "We've got some marvellous plays here! We've got wonderful talent here! We must give the public this talent!" If the public is asked what they want, you get a lot of waffle – you get a lot of quiz shows, you get a lot of chat shows, you certainly don't get drama.' Richard Digby Day concurs. 'Television has been disastrously limiting in audience taste.'

Audience taste may be limited, but it has become very powerful. Fifty years ago viewers were largely passive participants who were invited to send postcards to the BBC expressing their opinions. Under the lead of Mary Whitehouse some of them became active critics in the National Viewers' and Listeners' Association. But now, not only are they replacing artists in many popular shows, with the growth of interactive television they are encouraged to determine the content of programmes as well. No wonder many actors are nostalgic for the 'good old days'.

9

Ampexing – 'As Live'

THE ANECDOTES IN this book reveal how varied, unpredictable and often hair-raising it was to work on live broadcasts. The stories are representative of a relatively short period in the history of the medium, for by the end of the 1950s research was well under way into the development of equipment that could record material. Once the new system was introduced into this country, working practices within the studios began to change.

The experiments began with the use of filmed inserts. These were usually brief scenes shot using conventional 35mm film on locations outside the studio. During the live broadcast the action inside the studio would cease while the insert was fed into the programme by means of a process called telecine. Geoffrey Bayldon recalls the first time this occurred: 'I was in a play produced by Rudolf Cartier. It was the first live television play for both of us and the first time anyone had used film in a live television play. It was a small shot of an aeroplane landing. We all held our breath as they counted down to that moment, but it went OK.' Michael Kilgarriff also remembers telecine:

'There was filming on live television but only for exteriors, which were then put in as inserts. You would cut from the live studio over to telecine and then back, and of course the difference was enormous in the quality of the picture, but people accepted it in those days.' Peter Copley also remembers how obvious the change could be: 'In the early days studio recording and location recording were done on different sorts of cameras and the match was very bad.'

One of the producers on *Dixon of Dock Green* was able to make a slight improvement to the situation, says Peter Byrne. 'The filmed inserts were all done on 35mm film, which meant the contrast between that and the studio work was like day for night. If you were going to put it up on the big screen 35mm was necessary but 16mm, which was much cheaper and much easier, was much better in those circumstances and one of our producers, Ronnie Marsh, pioneered the use of it.'

Financial considerations were also behind the drive to experiment further with filming whole programmes, as BBC Enterprises, which was set up in the late sixties, discovered that there was money to be made from selling programmes to other networks. Leonard Lewis says that 'Right from the early *Z Cars*, Enterprises were selling them in a very limited way. Telerecording was very primitive. It involved pointing a film camera at the television screen, filming the programme and then developing it. If you were being telerecorded for BBC Enterprises, you would do some retakes at the end of the live transmissions, but basically the mistakes which had happened you had to put up with, the audience had seen them. There was no incentive to do retakes to get the show right just for Enterprises.' Peter Byrne reckons that the final product could not have been very impressive: 'Recording techniques were very crude. They were called telerecordings and they used to photograph the thing off the tube, so it was very dark and the sound balance was not very good.'

Clearly this was not an ideal situation, but a solution was found on the other side of the Atlantic, where American scientists invented what became known as the Ampex machine, an early version of the video camera.

The new technology was pioneered in this country by Rediffusion, and David London remembers his first encounter with it: 'On 24 June 1958 we had the first demonstration of the Ampex video recording machine which had come over from the States. Pictures and sound were recorded on a two-inch tape, it was a very wide tape. Each reel ran for sixty-four minutes. Editing was similar to filmediting, in that the tape had to be cut and spliced. It was cheaper than film because you could reuse the tape, provided it hadn't been edited. The quality was excellent. Initially programmes were still recorded as if they were live. They tried to avoid editing whenever they could because it wasn't very satisfactory. They tended to shoot whole scenes in one go and then stop, because it's easier to edit between scenes. The electronic editing that they do now came quite a lot later.'

Technician Roy Glew describes the tape: 'The early Ampex tape was two inches wide, they have now got it down to about half an inch. They are now able to get much more information on, so the tapes are shorter too. A one-hour Ampex tape would be about eighteen inches in diameter; they were massive great things and they were also very heavy.'

Economic factors appear to have influenced how the system was operated, according to Richard Bebb. 'When they started using Ampex it was incredibly expensive to cut and people were reluctant to do retakes. Actors got terribly nervous because it quickly became known that if you dried the Casting Department would not use you again.' Michael Kilgarriff is another who recalls dire warnings about stoppages: 'It was very expensive to edit. Figures varied, but we were told that it cost £200 a snip. It meant that you didn't have to do it live but you still had to do it in one go, as live. If there was a total cock-up, there was a chance of doing it again. The directors were very protect-ive of their budgets though, so if something went wrong and you asked to do it again they would say, "It'll be all right, it'll be all right." The stars got wise to this and if something went wrong they used to say, "Fuck!" '

Just what was involved is outlined by Bernard Hepton. 'The expensive part of Ampexing was the editing, because they used to do it with a razor blade. The old tape was about an inch and a half wide and the inch at the top of the tape was vision and the little bit underneath was sound, but the sound was never recorded at the same time as the vision – it was always a little later – so your razor blade had to do a little L. That was very skilful, the editors of those early tapes were very skilful indeed.' Leonard Lewis is able to add detail to this account. 'You'd record a scene and then stop, then you'd record another scene. When it was first introduced you were only allowed to stop about five times. When you went into the editing suite, you took that tape, the editor ran the tape until you told him to stop, he would put a bleep on it then he would take it off the machine and put it on to another one. He would then put iron filings on the tape which showed you the magnetic field, because there were edit pulse points on the tape and that was where you had to cut. If you edited anywhere else then the tape would jump. You took a razor blade and you cut the tape and then joined it on to the next bit, again using iron filings to make sure you had the right line. You virtually joined it with Sellotape and then you played the tape to make sure that it worked. If it didn't work then you took it off and did it again. It wasn't a very accurate system of editing. Each time you edited you went down a generation of tape and you lost quality until eventually it became untransmittable. Nowadays with digital you can get the same quality of the original.'

With so much at stake, Miriam Karlin comments wryly, 'They would stop the Ampex for something technical, something diabolical like a boom being in shot, but for actors – no.' Leonard Lewis provides an example of this principle at work. 'ITV was also going through the same process. Because it was a commercial company, I suspect there was even more pressure on them not to break the recording up and to keep going. They did one show, the climax of which was a man climbing along a high ridge. The high ridge they constructed in the studio was actually only a few inches off the floor. When they were recording this the actor climbing along the ridge fell off, but he got back on again and went on. At the end of the recording the floor manager, having got his instructions from the gallery, said, "Thank you, studio, no retakes." The poor actor went up to him and said, "You've got to retake it, I fell off!" After consulting the director, the floor manager said, "Don't worry, they can cut round it." When it was transmitted the actor sat at home, wondering how on earth they could possibly cut round it. He sits there watching it and just before it reaches the point where he fell off, the screen goes blank and a caption comes up: "Normal service will be resumed as soon as possible."'

Judy Campbell also recalls the ruthlessness of pressing ahead come what may: 'Cutting the tape was very, very expensive. I remember doing a Lonsdale play up in Yorkshire with Hugh Williams. We did it in twenties clothes and I was sent to Bermans and Nathans [theatrical costumiers]. I spent the whole day trying on dresses and saying, "Oh do let me have this one!" – choosing a dress just to go and post a letter! Of course, when it came to doing it, the costume changes really were difficult – little changing rooms had to be set up all over the place, it was a tremendous scramble – and I thought then what an idiot I was. We did have two breaks to change the set, but to have a break just because someone had forgotten their lines, or made a bit of a muddle about a move, was not popular at all because it was going to be costly. You pushed on in spite of the fact that you'd spilled your drink or whatever.'

This state of affairs appears to have continued for some time. Trevor Bannister started in television in 1960. 'I remember doing *Emergency Ward 10* where you rehearsed two episodes: one went out live and you then did the next episode which was recorded on a system which was called Ampexing.' Other actors also recall that early episodes of *Crossroads* were done in this manner, one going out live and one recorded on the same day. Stephen Hancock started playing Ernie Bishop in *Coronation Street* in about 1959 and says, 'I seem to remember that it was recorded, but you did it all in a lump, you didn't do it scene by scene as you do now. You did the entire show from beginning to end and if there were any bad bits you could do little retakes, which they inserted.' Leslie Lawton corroborates Hancock's recollection: '*Coronation Street* was Ampexed to start with. If you made a mistake you never went back. If you said a line wrong they put an aeroplane over it, or something. You never, ever did a retake. It was done as live. You ran from one set to the other with the tape still running.'

Peter Copley believes this system was detrimental to the production. 'For many years there was a transition period when television was no longer live, when plays were no longer necessarily performed uninterruptedly; you did one scene at a time and that seemed like death. I remember thinking *If only they could film it, do it exactly like film, or do it like a live play*, but the intermediate [method] was deadening to perform and deadening to the ultimate product. Sometimes it was terrifying: you'd get to the end of a shooting day and there were still three scenes to do. You would record a scene from beginning to end and think that it was terrible and then you'd hear from the box, "Excellent, excellent!" You knew it was simply because they were running out of time.'

However, according to Margaret Tyzack there were benefits to working with Ampex. 'In the early days of recording you were able to play a whole scene right through, rather than in snatched sentences. That gave you the feeling of being more in control. It wasn't soundbite drama; you were able to follow things through.'

For actors who found the terror of working entirely live unendurable, the arrival of the Ampex machine must have been a godsend. Wendy Craig states, 'I don't honestly think that doing live television is any improvement in any way. Some people think you get a much more exciting performance; I think you get a terrified performance.' Bernard Hepton supports this point of view. 'There was a faction of people who fundamentally believed that live performances were much more alive than recorded ones. I disagree with this, because the nerves are still there are in front of a camera, you don't suddenly relax. You know that you can do it again, but if you have to do it again you feel a berk.' George Baker believes, 'We've lost nothing by losing the immediacy of doing it on the night. There's just no point in doing things live, it's so good the way it is now. I'm sure the actor has more fun in a way [when live], but I don't think it's so good for the audience.'

While everybody involved in television was gradually getting to grips with the implications of recording performances rather than broadcasting them live, other technological developments were coming on apace. On 21 April 1964, following the recommendation of the Pilkington report two years earlier, BBC 2 was launched on to the airwaves. At that time broadcasting took place on VHF using 405 lines and in order to bring Britain into harmony with the European standard the new channel was broadcast on UHF using 625 lines, giving greater visual definition. At its launch it was only available in London and the south-east, but by the spring of 1965 the new transmitter at Sutton Coldfield made the

BBC's second channel available throughout the Midlands. However the public was slow to take to BBC 2 because of its limited availability and also because new television sets were needed in order to receive it.

The launch was intended to take place on 20 April, but in fact happened a day later. Bernard Hepton explains why. 'At the opening of BBC 2, there were an awful lot of electricity strikes around the country. Everybody was geared to the opening of BBC 2 and on the first night there was an electricity strike. Everybody was in the bar, the management were there with champagne, and nothing happened, there was an absolute black-out. Some people were laughing, some people were crying, but the candles came out and it turned into a really wonderful party.'

The change from 405 lines to 625 enabled the introduction of another recommendation made by the Pilkington Committee, that colour transmissions should be brought on stream as soon as possible. A number of systems from America, Germany and France were experimented with, delaying the start of this new technology until 1967. From 1 July that year, BBC 2 was allowed to broadcast in colour for five hours a week on an experimental basis, and made a point of including plenty of verdant coverage of the Wimbledon Tennis Championships to seduce the public into buying the necessary sets. These cost about £200, roughly equivalent to £1,500 today. This was not the only expense, as the licence fee was increased to a hefty £10 to cover the cost of the new invention. On 2 December 1967 the experiment ended and the colour service was officially started on that channel, but colour transmissions were not available to the whole country until 1969.

Josephine Tewson remembers her first experience of working in colour. 'There was a pioneering feel when colour came in. I was doing sketches in a show with Charlie Drake and he especially wrote material that could take advantage of it. There was one sketch about a decorator and I was playing the house owner and he ended up throwing pots of different-coloured paint all over the walls.' Geoffrey Bayldon recalls, 'I played the White Knight in *Alice in Wonderland*, which was shot with a colour overlay, which meant that everything had to be blue, so that the colour could be superimposed on it. Even the bucket on standby in case my horse peed was blue.'

Working in colour had an effect on the way Peter Byrne performed his long-running role in *Dixon of Dock Green*: 'We were one of the first programmes to go into colour. My performance changed with the advent of colour. Before that we used lots of light, which produced masses of heat. When colour came in, it was more the intensity of light . . . I suddenly started to squint and the newspapers said, "He's become a hard-eyed cop." That was because the light was so bright I couldn't see.'

Leslie Lawton describes another side-effect of the introduction of the new service: 'Doing a programme in colour took so much longer than anything I'd ever done in black and white [being technically more complex]. I remember standing about for an hour just while they lined up a credit shot. A lot of directors didn't like it because they thought it slowed things down. They thought it was really bad for comedy because it made it slower.'

The same year that saw the launch of BBC 2 also witnessed the first public demonstration of a home video recorder. This happened at Alexandra Palace. A recording was made of the opening of the *Nine o'Clock News* and the tape was played back to the viewers later in the bulletin. Another notable technological breakthrough that occurred during the 1960s was the ability to broadcast via satellite. This first took place in July 1962 when live pictures from America were transmitted via the Telstar satellite to sixteen European countries. Television had begun to shrink the world.

This flurry of technical progress during the mid to late 1960s represents something of a watershed in the history of television. The change from transmitting live programmes to broadcasting as live, and ultimately to recording, combined with other innovations like colour photography, were all instrumental in transforming the medium from something that was largely derived from the theatre into something that more closely resembled the cinema, both in the process of production and in the end result. Live television particularly lent itself to the performance of single plays that could be done and dusted in one sitting, and many actors mourn the disappearance of this kind of work. Ian Flintoff believes that the popularity of soap operas has effectively sidelined individual dramas: 'There is a great desire among actors for the return of the single play to television. Both actors and writers and directors feel that the single television play was and should be a marvellous piece of television creativity. Now, with long-running series and serials, the main task is to keep a good storyline going.'

The historian Andrew Crisell suggests that single drama is more costly to make than soaps, and harder to sell abroad, thus rendering it economically unviable. George Baker also identifies the need to make a profit as a stumbling block. 'I've done 108 television plays and it was just as stable as the theatre in many ways. There were so many productions going on, but I'm sorry to say Mrs Thatcher did us no favours when she put us into the bidding stakes and the hands of the shareholder, because the shareholder has to have a return or he will put his money somewhere else. So the real excitement has gone. I'm not saying that the good times have gone, what I'm saying is that the old well-made television play has gone.'

Epilogue

WITH THE BENEFIT of hindsight, many artists seem to think that working practices now compare unfavourably with the earliest days when programmes stood or fell, but went out live. Peter Bowles says: 'It was very exciting, it's dull by comparison now.' David Hamilton also misses the excitement of the old days. 'A lot of the fun has gone out of television, a lot of the spontaneity. Television now is predictable, it plays safe. The fun was infectious; if you had fun the viewers had fun watching.'

Occasional attempts have been made to recapture the excitement of a live broadcast. Sheila Reid recalls the sensation when this kind of experiment took place. 'I only did one live television show, a *Z Cars*. The BBC had in fact been producing them for some time *not* live, but the regulars had (in the BBC's eyes at least) become somewhat lackadaisical and lacklustre and so they decided to frighten them into their old sense of urgency by shooting our episode live. Hundreds of tiny scenes, everyone dashing from set to set, and indeed *very* frightening! But not, of course, for the regulars: they were calm and assured and phlegmatic as ever, it was the rest of us who were thrown into total panic. There was certainly an added frisson, looking back.' One of the assured and phlegmatic regulars, Colin Welland, disliked the recorded programmes of the long-running police series. 'Some of the episodes were recorded to give us a break, if they were going to go out on Christmas Day or something, and when they were recorded we went to pieces because there was no adrenalin, and they had to do take after take.'

Another attempt to rediscover what it was like to broadcast drama live was undertaken in the early 1980s. Michael Cochrane explains what happened. 'In 1983 Robin Midgley was Head of Drama at BBC Pebble Mill. He thought it would be a good idea to resurrect the notion of live drama. He commissioned six plays of about forty-five minutes or an hour's duration. We spent three weeks rehearsing it and five weeks laughing. The idea was that it would heighten the tension for the audience and they would get more pleasure from watching it. Whether this was the case, or whether it just heightened the tension for the actors, I don't know. I had a lot of words to say and then I stopped and handed over to Norman Beeton for a bit. I had to sit in a deck-chair and pretend to go to sleep. I remember thinking as I closed my eyes, *Phew! Thank God! I've got through half of this damn thing and now all I've got to do is to sit here for four minutes while Norman does the bunny* [rabbits on]. While I was sitting there I was thinking that there were probably four million people watching this. Well, I was wrong, there were actually four people watching it and three of those were my agent and parents! When I first started in 1967, the older generation of actors were always talking about live television and live radio – "Until you've done live television you're not really an actor" – so it was a great thing to have done. It's not a thing I would particularly like to repeat; I'm not quite sure of the validity of it. You have a one-and-only chance to get things right for the director and the writer, not like in the theatre when you can do it again and again. If it went horribly wrong, there you were, stranded. They didn't have a prompter or anything. Norman had a great idea: if he dried he was just going to laugh that manic laugh of his and wait until somebody said something. I had a great big box of tricks containing the Bible and Shakespeare, so Jeffrey [Kissoon] decided that if he dried he would rummage about in this, pick out a book and read from it. Chris Asanti and I didn't know what we would do, we thought we might dance!' Bernard Hepton was one of the 'four' people watching. 'About ten years ago there was a director who wanted to do live plays from Birmingham. I saw a couple of them and you could actually see the terror in the actors' eyes, the angst, the nerves.'

Both Barbara Lott and George Baker were involved in a similar venture and offer accounts of what the experience was like. 'About twenty years ago as a gimmick Thames Television did six half-hour plays live. I was in one with George Baker. It was rather frightening doing a live play again after all those years, particularly as George had terrible flu and we didn't know if we would get through it. It was a two-hander and when we got down to the floor I looked round and all the cameramen were rather white and shaking. One man appeared to be on his knees in prayer. Anyhow, it all went very well and afterwards up in the bar I remember one of them saying, "It was marvellous. When I couldn't quite get into that position and you realized it and moved a little to the left, I'd never before felt so involved! I felt part of the show." '

In Baker's recollection the flu seems to have been a minor preoccupation; quite literally, he had other fish to fry. 'Later on somebody decided it would be a wonderful idea to do three live television programmes. They offered me a wonderful script playing a bank clerk looking after his elderly mother . . . He comes in from the office and he has brought fish fingers and this and that and the other . . . Then came the great moment when we were going to do it, and I walked on, chat, chat, chat, chat, over to the stove, turned on the gas, struck a light – no gas. Struck another light, no gas. Thank God one of the props men had actually stayed on the floor (they usually go off into the props room and sit down and have a cup of tea). He saw what was happening, went over to the Calor gas cylinder and turned it on. It threw our timings a little but we got through it.'

Colin Welland also pays homage to the early crews. 'I look back at live television with great fondness. You couldn't do it now – the technicians couldn't do it any more. The cameramen were highly trained at shooting across the studio, focusing as they went and arriving at their line on time. There was lots of trust between the cameramen and the actors. It was like a university of television, a marvellous education in screen acting.'

Although the single play is less of a feature in current schedules, in the drama that survives some would argue that there has been a significant improvement in the standard of acting. This can be put down to enhanced training, but could also suggest that live performance was stressful and inhibiting for the actor. Ian Carmichael is full of praise for current achievements: 'I look at television these days and see some very good young actors. They are now absolutely trained and attuned to doing work to a television camera, they know that they must do practically nothing, that they mustn't be histrionic. They all want to be on television because that is the going medium, that is the medium that is making stars.'

Yet perhaps today's performers are reaping the benefit of the pioneering work undertaken by their predecessors, who hammered out a new style of acting in the most adverse conditions. The producers, writers, directors and technicians involved in the early days had to surmount their own inexperience and invent a whole new vocabulary of creative expression. Collectively their work has reshaped the social, domestic and artistic landscape of the twentieth century.

Contributors

Dame Eileen Atkins

Dame Eileen Atkins began her career at the Open Air Theatre in Regents Park before going on to work at the RSC in Stratford-upon-Avon, at the Old Vic and the National Theatre. She appeared in *Semi-Detached* with Laurence Olivier and *Exit the King* with Alec Guinness, and in 1965 won the Evening Standard Award for Best Actress in *The Killing of Sister George*. Subsequently she won a Variety Club award for her role as Elizabeth in *Vivat! Vivat! Regina!*. She has received Olivier Awards as Best Supporting Actress in *The Winter's Tale* and as Best Actress in *The Unexpected Man*. Eileen's television credits include leading roles in *The Three Sisters*, *The Heiress*, *Olive* and *The Letter*, and the title roles in *Major Barbara*, *The Duchess of Malfi*, *Electra*, *The Lady from the Sea* and *The Jean Rhys Woman*. Her film appearances include *The Dresser*, *Equus*, *Let Him Have It*, *Jack and Sarah* and most recently *Gosford Park*.

George Baker

Best known for his role as Inspector Wexford in *The Ruth Rendell Mysteries*, George Baker began his career in repertory theatre before moving on to the West End, where he has appeared in twenty-seven productions. His considerable film career includes roles in *The*

Dambusters, *Moonraker*, *Goodbye Mr Chips*, *On Her Majesty's Secret Service*, *The Spy Who Loved Me* and *The Thirty Nine Steps*. He has appeared in one hundred and eight television plays, most notably as Emperor Tiberius in *I, Claudius*. He has worked extensively as a director and a writer – he starred in his own comedy series, *Bowler* – and has had his poetry broadcast on *Poets Today* and *Poetry Now* for the BBC.

Trevor Bannister

Trevor Bannister has wide experience of working in regional theatre, both on tour and in rep. He has made a particular special-ity of playing pantomime dames, with over fifteen to his credit. His many West End appearances include *The Odd Couple*, *Move Over Mrs Markham* and *Billy Liar*. His best-known television role was as Mr Lucas in *Are You Being Served?* He has also appeared in numerous other productions, amongst them *The Upper Hand*, *Cider with Rosie*, *The Saint*, *Voyage Round My Father* and *Country Matters*.

Venetia Barrett

Venetia Barrett has toured in both India and the UK and has worked in a number of repertory companies. She played Mme de Rosemonde in the world tour of the RSC's *Les Liaisons dangereuses* and appeared in *The Mousetrap* in the West End. Amongst her television appearances are *Inspector Morse*, *Wish Me Luck* and *The House of Eliott*. She has also been seen in Jon Amiel's film *The Man Who Knew Too Little*.

Geoffrey Bayldon

Geoffrey Bayldon has extensive experience of working in live television. Among his many credits are appearances in the *Brass Band Comedies*, written by Willis Hall, *Alice in Wonderland* and *The Case of the Frightened Lady*.

Richard Bebb

Richard Bebb began his career in repertory, including working with Michael Redgrave at the Embassy Theatre in Swiss Cottage. He has appeared in over a thousand radio plays, sharing the narration with Richard Burton in the original radio production of Dylan Thomas's *Under Milk Wood*. He has also been seen in over a hundred television productions including *Z Cars*, *Softly Softly*, *Madame Curie*, *The Barchester Chronicles*, *A Question of Attribution*, *Little Lord Fauntleroy* and *Cold Comfort Farm*. He regularly writes obituaries for the *Independent*, is a leading authority on the pronunciation of Middle English and lectures on theatrical and operatic subjects at various universities including Leicester, Yale, Princeton, Columbia and the Smithsonian Institute.

Peter Birrel

Among Peter Birrel's recent work is his appearance as Costas in *London's Burning*. He has also been seen on tour in *Love Letters*.

Peter Bowles

Peter Bowles is best-known for his work on television, which numbers successes such as *Isadora*, *The Crezz*, *Rumpole of the Bailey*, *To the Manor Born*, *The Irish R.M.*, *The Bounders*, *Lytton's Diary* and *Perfect Scoundrels*. He has appeared in repertory and the West End, where recent credits include *Present Laughter* and *School for Wives*.

Faith Brook

Faith Brook has made film appearances in *Elgar's Tenth Muse* and *North Sea Hijack*. Among numerous roles on television in both Britain and America, she played Lady Knox in *The Irish R.M.* She has also worked extensively with the National Theatre, the RSC and in the West End.

Peter Byrne

Peter Byrne was a stalwart of live television, appearing in *The Pattern of Marriage* with Billie Whitelaw early in his career, and going on to fame for his twenty-year portrayal of Sergeant Andy Crawford in the hugely popular *Dixon of Dock Green*. He has worked in repertory and appeared in the West End in *Boeing-Boeing* and *There's a Girl in My Soup*, and has also worked in Canada.

Adrian Cairns

Adrian Cairns began his career as an actor in television before being invited to join the newly established Tyne Tees Television as an announcer and newsreader. After many years in television he returned to his theatrical roots, working as an associate director of the Old Vic Theatre School in Bristol.

Judy Campbell

Judy Campbell first worked in the theatre in 1937, appearing in repertory and subsequently the West End. During the war she toured with Noël Coward in *This Happy Breed*, *Present Laughter* and *Blithe Spirit*. She has been seen in a wide range of television productions, including *The Upper Hand*, *The House of Eliott* and *Bergerac*. Recently she appeared in *Remembrance of Things Past* at the National Theatre, in the series *Armadillo* for BBC 1, and in Granada's adaptation of *The Forsyte Saga*.

Ian Carmichael

Ian Carmichael first appeared on stage at the People's Palace, Mile End, in 1939. During the war he served in the 22nd Dragoons and resumed his career with many appearances on television before making his mark on stage in *The Lyric Review* in 1951. Other theatre work includes *Boeing-Boeing* in New York, *Getting Married*, *The Circle*, *School for Scandal* and co-starring with Deborah Kerr in Peter

Ustinov's play *Overheard*. He is best-known for his portrayal of Bertie Wooster and Lord Peter Wimsey in two long-running BBC series.

Constance Chapman

Constance Chapman began her career in repertory companies in Nottingham, Manchester and Bristol, but has also worked with the RSC both in this country and abroad, at the Royal Court and in the West End. On television she has been seen in several productions including *The Farmer's Wife*, *The Gorge* and *School for Scandal*, and among her films are *The Raging Moon*, *Hedda Gabler* and *A Day in the Death of Joe Egg*.

Maria Charles

Maria Charles came to prominence in the original production of *The Boyfriend*, since when she has made many West End appearances, amongst them *Annie* and *Fiddler on the Roof*. She has worked at the National Theatre, in repertory and on the London fringe. On television she was nominated for a BAFTA award for her performance in *Bar Mitzvah Boy* and has been in numerous other productions including *La Ronde*, *Country Matters*, *Brideshead Revisited* and *Shine on Harvey Moon*. Among her film credits are *Great Expectations*, *Revenge of the Pink Panther* and *Victor/Victoria*.

Michael Cochrane

Michael Cochrane's long and varied television career includes leading roles in *Wings*, *Love in a Cold Climate*, *The Citadel* and *Fortunes of War*. He has also been seen in *The Two Ronnies*, *Shelley*, *The Darling Buds of May*, *Keeping Up Appearances*, *Heartbeat* and *Longitude*. He has worked in the West End, at the Old Vic and the Chichester Festival and in many other regional theatres. Amongst his film credits are *Escape to Victory*, *Return of the Soldier* and *The Far Pavilions*.

George Cole

George Cole began his career in the provinces at the Grand, Blackpool, in 1939. He has starred in countless West End shows, amongst them *Hedda Gabler*, *Too True To Be Good* and *The Philanthropist*. Best-known for his role as Arthur Daley in *Minder*, he has also appeared in *A Life of Bliss*, *Blackmail*, *A Man of our Times*, *The Gold Robbers*, *Don't Forget to Write*, *The Voyage of Charles Darwin*, *The Bounder* and *Blott on the Landscape*.

Peter Copley

Peter Copley has lengthy experience of working in repertory, particularly at the Bristol Old Vic. He has also worked on the London fringe, in the West End and for the RSC. On television he has been in *Wives and Daughters*, *Jonathan Creek*, *Lovejoy*, *One Foot in the Grave*, *The Prisoner of Zenda*, *Churchill and the Generals* and *Far From the Madding Crowd*. He has appeared in several films, most notably *Empire of the Sun*.

Wendy Craig

Wendy Craig has worked in repertory, at the Chichester Festival, in many West End successes and on Broadway. Her London theatre credits include *George Dillon*, *A Resounding Tinkle*, *Sport of My Mad Mother*, *Beyond Reasonable Doubt* and recently *The Rivals* for the RSC. She has been in many films, amongst them *Room at the Top*, *Joseph Andrews* and *The Servant*, for which she was nominated for a BAFTA award. She has appeared in a number of top TV comedy series including *Not in Front of the Children*, *Nanny*, *And Mother Makes Three*, *Mother Makes Five*, *Butterflies* and *Brighton Belles*. Kenneth Tynan once described her as 'one of the six best young actresses in the Western world', and other accolades include a BAFTA award for TV Drama Actress of the Year, the Variety Club of Great Britain award for Personality of the Year and BBC TV's Woman of the Year. She was also voted the Funniest Woman on Television for three consecutive years by readers of the *TV Times*.

Maurice Denham

Maurice Denham first worked in rep at Hull in 1934. He saw active service during the war and was also associated with the famous radio programme *ITMA*. From 1946 until 1949 he could be heard regularly on the radio in *Much Binding in the Marsh*. He worked at the Old Vic, the Royal Court and in the West End. Among his many television credits are *Talking to a Stranger*, *The Lotus Eaters*, *Fall of Eagles*, *The Old Men at the Zoo*, *The Bill* and *Pie in the Sky*. His films include *The Chain* and *84 Charing Cross Road*. He died in 2002.

Richard Digby Day

Richard Digby Day has been director of five regional theatres, including Exeter and Nottingham. He also ran the Open Air Theatre in Regents Park, and lectures extensively in America. He is a fellow of the Royal Society of Arts.

Tom Edwards

In the early stages of his career Tom Edwards worked in pirate radio, first for Radio City and then for Radio Caroline. He went on to become the youngest ever newsreader and presenter, working for Anglia Television on *Look East*. He has also worked as a disc jockey on BBC Radio's *Midday Spin*.

Malcolm Farquhar

Malcolm Farquhar has a distinguished career in regional theatre – he was resident director at Cheltenham, Worthing and Bristol and has staged productions at Basingstoke, Birmingham and Northampton. As an actor he has made many West End appearances: *A Woman of No Importance*, *The Boston Story*, *Highly Confidential*, *Lady Frederick* and *Winnie the Pooh*. He has toured extensively throughout the country and his television work includes Major Booty in *The Riff Raff Element*.

Contributors

Ian Flintoff

Ian Flintoff has worked for the National Theatre, the RSC and the Royal Court. On television he has appeared in *Brookside*, *Casualty*, *Boon*, *London's Burning*, *The House of Eliott*, *Prime Suspect*, *A Touch of Frost* and *Coronation Street*. As a writer his work has been published, staged and also broadcast by the BBC.

Roy Glew

Roy Glew began work in the 1950s as a trainee technician at the BBC, where he learned all aspects of sound engineering, camera maintenance and lighting. He remained with the Corporation for many years.

James Grout

One of James Grout's first appearances in the West End was in *Half a Sixpence*, which won him a Tony nomination during its run on Broadway. He has played Chief Superintendent Strange throughout the series of *Inspector Morse* and among his other television credits are *David Copperfield*, *Goodnight Sweetheart*, *Drop the Dead Donkey*, *Rumpole of the Bailey*, *Northern Lights*, *A Very Peculiar Practice*, *Yes, Minister* and *All Creatures Great and Small*.

David Hamilton

David Hamilton is well known for his work as a radio DJ and television presenter. He started his career writing continuity scripts for ATV before joining British Forces Network Radio in Germany, after which he was one of the first continuity announcers for ABC Television in Manchester. From here he joined Tyne Tees Television. For many years he was a popular DJ on Radios 1 and 2, and also worked as a presenter on *Top of the Pops*.

Stephen Hancock

Known for his eight-year-long portrayal of Ernie Bishop in *Coronation Street*, Stephen Hancock has made dozens of appearances on television, including an eighteen-month stint on *Emergency Ward 10*. He has worked in the West End, for the RSC and in repertory. As a musician he has done orchestration and arranging for London City Ballet, Scottish Opera and the RSC.

Janet Hargreaves

Janet Hargreaves is best remembered as Rosemary Hunter in *Crossroads*, but has many other television roles to her credit, including Dr Cheryl Barnes in *The Doctors* and parts in *Poirot*, *Hetty Wainthropp Investigates*, *Dr Who* and *Voyage Round My Father*. She has appeared on stage in the West End, the London fringe, Los Angeles and in rep. Her film work includes *The Deadly Affair* directed by Sydney Lumet and *Frankenstein and the Monster From Hell*.

Sir Nigel Hawthorne

The late Sir Nigel Hawthorne won more than sixteen prestigious awards both here and abroad for his work on stage and in the cinema. He was nominated for an Oscar for his performance in *The Madness of King George* and in 1996 was given the Gold Medal of Honour by the National Arts Club of New York. His theatre work included *King Lear*, *The Madness of George III*, *Shadowlands*, *Peer Gynt*, *Privates on Parade* and several productions at the Royal Court, including *West of Suez* and *A Sense of Detachment* by John Osborne. On television he was seen in countless productions, amongst them *The Fragile Heart*, *Relatively Speaking*, *The Barchester Chronicles* and *Mapp and Lucia*. It is as Sir Humphrey Appleby in *Yes, Minister* and *Yes, Prime Minister* that he will be best remembered.

Bernard Hepton

Bernard Hepton has comprehensive first-hand knowledge of the theatre and television. He worked as an actor in repertory at York, Manchester, Bromley, Bristol, Guildford, Scarborough and Birmingham, where he was also artistic director for four years. In television he worked not only as an actor but also as a producer and director. His best-known role is probably as the Kommandant in *Colditz*, but he also appeared as Cranmer in *The Six Wives of Henry VIII*, in *Middlemarch*, *The Scarlet Pimpernel*, *A Pin to See the Peepshow*, *Secret Army*, *Tinker, Tailor, Soldier, Spy*, *Smiley's People*, *The Charmer* and *Midsomer Murders*. His films include *The Six Wives of Henry VIII*, *Barry Lyndon*, *Get Carter* and most recently *Emma*.

Donald Hewlett

Probably best-known for his portrayal of Colonel Reynolds in *It Ain't Half Hot Mum*, Donald Hewlett has numerous television appearances to his credit, amongst them *You Rang, M'Lord?* and *Lovejoy*. He was also seen as M in the Bond film *Goldeneye*.

Bob Holness

Bob Holness began his career in South Africa, working in repertory and then for the South African Broadcasting Corporation, where he played the first ever James Bond, in a radio version of *Moonraker*. On his return to Britain he presented the quiz show *Take a Letter* for Granada and was involved in *World in Action*, *What The Papers Say* and *Breakthrough* as a reporter, interviewer, announcer and newsreader. In 1967 he co-presented the TV news magazine *Today*, while presenting *Top of the Form* on Radio 4. For eight and a half years he was presenter of *Late Night Extra* on Radio 2 and for ten years joint presenter of LBC's award-winning *A.M. Show*. Holness created the music/anthology programme *Anything Goes*, which ran for twenty-two years on the BBC World Service. He was the host of *Blockbusters*, which garnered six BAFTA nominations. He is currently chairman of *Call My Bluff*.

Glyn Houston

Glyn Houston has wide experience of regional theatre, including seasons at Chichester and Theatr Clwyd. He first worked in television in 1948 and amongst his credits are *The Beach Inspector*, *The Keep*, *The Bill*, *Old Scores* and *Trouble Makers*. He has also been seen in more than sixty films.

David Jacobs

David Jacobs started his broadcasting career in the Royal Navy during the war, serving on the staff of Lord Mountbatten as Chief Announcer on Radio SEAC in Ceylon. When demobilized, he joined the BBC as an announcer and newsreader. His major radio credits include *Housewives' Choice*, *Pick of the Pops*, *Any Questions?* and *Any Answers?*. He was a founder member of Capital Radio. On television he has hosted *Juke Box Jury*, *Top of the Pops*, *What's My Line?*, *The Eurovision Song Contest*, *Miss World* and *Come Dancing*. He currently presents *The David Jacobs Collection* on Radio 2. In 1984 he was the recipient of the Sony Gold Award for outstanding contribution to radio over the years, and in 1996 he was created a CBE.

Edward Jewesbury

Edward Jewesbury has worked in rep as well as with Kenneth Branagh's Renaissance Theatre Company, the RSC and at Chichester. On television he has recently been seen in *Kavanagh QC* and *Hildegard*, and his films include *Peter's Friends*, *Much Ado About Nothing* and *Beautiful People*.

Miriam Karlin

Miriam Karlin's best-known television part was Paddy in *The Rag Trade*, but she has also been seen in *Doctors*, *Holby City* and *Casualty*. Among her films are Stanley Kubrick's *A Clockwork Orange*. She has worked in numerous reps and at the Chichester Festival Theatre.

She has also appeared at the Royal Court, the Almeida, the Young Vic, the RSC and in the West End. She has served as an Equity delegate to the TUC and was awarded an OBE for her services to the theatre.

Mary Kenton

Mary Kenton has a wide experience of working in repertory, including several seasons as a leading lady in Northampton. Among her television credits are *Family Solicitor*, *The Sullavan Brothers*, *The Newcomers* and *Mrs Thursday*. She has also published a volume of poetry.

Michael Kilgarriff

Michael Kilgarriff has worked in numerous repertory companies, has been seen in thirty-five pantomimes and for thirty-four years has wielded the gavel as chairman of the world-famous Players Theatre Music Hall in London. On television he has appeared in *Dr Who*, *Without Walls* and *Tales From the Map Room*. As a member of the BBC Radio Repertory Company he worked on *Cyrano de Bergerac* with Ralph Richardson, *Othello* with Paul Schofield, *The Dales* and *The Archers*. He is an international best-selling author of books on music hall, popular song and comedy.

Harry Landis

Known to many as Felix in *EastEnders*, Harry Landis has appeared in several hundred television series, amongst them *Minder*, *A Woman of Substance*, *Bergerac*, *Lovejoy*, *Howard's Way* and *Sherlock Holmes*. He has worked at the Birmingham Rep, the Manchester Royal Exchange and in many other regional theatres, and has also been seen at the National Theatre and in the West End.

Contributors

Leslie Lawton

Leslie Lawton worked as a child actor for ABC Television in Manchester, which later led to work in *Coronation Street*. He has numerous television and theatre roles to his credit and has served as artistic director of theatre companies at Westcliff-on-Sea, Liverpool and Edinburgh.

Christopher Lee

During the Second World War Christopher Lee served in the Royal Air Force and Special Forces. He held the rank of flight lieutenant and was decorated for distinguished service. After demobilization he started working in films and is listed in the *Guinness Book of World Records* as being the international star with the most screen credits. The best-known of these are *A Tale of Two Cities*, *Dracula*, *The Wicker Man*, *The Private Life of Sherlock Holmes*, *The Man with the Golden Gun* and *The Lord of the Rings*. He has worked with numerous directors including John Houston, Joseph Losey, Orson Welles, Michael Powell, Billy Wilder and Steven Spielberg. He has received awards for his contribution to the cinema from the United States, France, Germany, Spain and Great Britain. He is the author of a number of books – his autobiography *Tall, Dark and Gruesome*, *The Great Villains*, *Archives of Evil* and *The Films of Christopher Lee*.

Leonard Lewis

Leonard Lewis began his career in repertory before crossing over into the world of television, where he worked first as an assistant floor manager and eventually as both a director and producer. He directed many episodes of *Z Cars* and its successor *Softly Softly*, as well as a huge number of individual television plays.

Contributors

David London

David London was a stage manager in the theatre before being recruited by independent television when it first went on air. He was involved behind the scenes on many productions, including Fanny Craddock's cookery show, and he worked for several years broadcasting racing on Channel 4.

Barbara Lott

Barbara Lott appeared regularly opposite Ronnie Corbett in the comedy series *Sorry* and as Auntie Pearl in *2.4 Children*. Her other television credits include *Nana*, *War and Peace*, *Ballet Shoes*, *The Duchess of Duke Street*, *The Trial of Lady Chatterley*, *Sexton Blake* and *Inspector Morse: The Remorseful Day*. She has been seen in repertory companies at Harrogate, Barnsley and Brighton and made her first appearance in London in John Gielgud's production of *Love For Love*. She has appeared in a number of films, amongst them *The Pillow Book* directed by Peter Greenaway.

Phillip Manikum

Phillip Manikum has worked extensively in repertory and also appeared in Peter Brook's legendary production of *A Midsummer Night's Dream* for the RSC. On television he has been seen in *Mme Bovary*, *Dalziel and Pascoe*, *The Young Indiana Jones*, *The Bill*, *Peak Practice* and *EastEnders*. He regularly tours in his own one-man show, *Scouting For Boys*.

Keith Martin

Keith Martin began his career on pirate radio. He was employed as a presenter by ABC in Manchester when independent television was launched.

Hilary Mason

Hilary Mason's considerable work in the theatre has been comple-
mented by a list of television credits that includes *An Independent
Man, Casualty, One Foot in the Grave, Nelson's Column* and *Love Hurts*. In
films she played Heather in *Don't Look Now* and the Medium in
Haunted.

Alec McCowen

Alec McCowen began his career in rep at Macclesfield, but soon
moved on to the West End and Broadway. He has done seasons
with the Old Vic and the RSC, for whom he toured the USSR as
the Fool in Peter Brook's *King Lear*. He has twice won the Evening
Standard Best Actor Award and once the Variety Club award for
Best Actor. Among his films are *The Cruel Sea, Frenzy, Travels With
My Aunt* and *The Age of Innocence*.

Peggy Mount

After working in repertory for fifteen years, Peggy Mount shot to
fame in *Sailor Beware*, which ran for three years in the West End and
was also filmed. Her stage work included seasons at the Old Vic,
the National and the RSC and among her films were *The Naked
Truth, Hotel Paradiso, Inn For Trouble, One Way Pendulum* and *Ladies Who
Do*. Her performance as Ada in *The Larkins* which was screened live
on television from 1958 until 1964 won her a wide popular following. She was awarded the OBE for her services to the theatre. She
died in 2001.

Brian Murphy

For many years Brian Murphy was a member of Joan Littlewood's
Theatre Workshop at Stratford East and created the roles he played
in *Oh, What a Lovely War!* and *The Hostage*. His television credits are
numerous but he is probably best-known as George Roper in *Man*

About the House and *George and Mildred*, and more recently amongst the very young for his work on *Wizadora*. In London he has appeared at the Almeida, the Young Vic and in the West End, and has also toured extensively and worked in many regional theatre companies.

Richard O'Callaghan

Richard O'Callaghan has an impressive number of theatre credits, including work at the Royal Exchange, the National, the RSC, the Chichester Festival, the Young Vic and the Royal Court. On television he has been seen in *Z Cars*, *Vile Bodies*, *Churchill's People*, *Professional Foul*, *Paying Guests*, *Boon*, *Hannay* and *Casualty*. Amongst his films are *Watership Down*, *Galileo*, *Butley* and *The Bofors Gun*.

Roger Ostime

Roger Ostime began his career in Fit-Up Theatre with the Garrick Players, who were based in Newton Poppleford, Devon. He worked extensively in rep and has made several television appearances, in *Stolen*, *Countdown to War*, *Capital City* and *Lovejoy*.

Norman Painting

Writer and broadcaster Norman Painting has the unique distinction of appearing in *The Guinness Book of Records* for his portrayal of Phil Archer in Radio 4's *The Archers* for over fifty years. The son of a railwayman, he studied at Oxford and became a Fellow of the University. He is a prolific writer as well as broadcaster and amongst his publications is *Forever Ambridge*.

Eve Pearce

Eve Pearce has been seen in numerous television programmes, including *Midsomer Murders*, *Poirot*, *Taggart*, *Thomas and Sarah*,

A Fine Romance and *Lytton's Diary*. She is widely experienced in the theatre – among her credits are appearances at the RSC, the National, the Almeida, the Gate and the Royal Court – and her many films include *Reunion at Fairborough, Bloody Sunday* and *Please Sir*.

Sheila Reid

Sheila Reid was a founder member of the noted Actors Company and in 1963 won Most Promising Actress of the Year for her performance in *The Gentle Avalanche* at the Royal Court. Since then she has appeared at the National, the RSC, the Old Vic, the Almeida and the Chichester Festival. Her many television credits include *Dr Finlay's Casebook, Auf Wiedersehen, Pet, Home Front, Fame Is the Spur, Love Among the Artists, All Creatures Great and Small* and *The Sweeney*. She has recently been seen in the film *Winter Guest* and in the musical *Martin Guerre*.

Paul Rogers

Highlights of Paul Rogers' distinguished career in the theatre have been his winning of the Clarence Derwent Award for his portrayal of William Villon in *The Other Heart* at the Old Vic in 1952, and a Tony Award on Broadway in 1967 for *The Homecoming*. On television he has appeared in *The Three Sisters, The Skin Game* and *A Tragedy of Two Ambitions*, and his films include *Billy Budd, The Homecoming* and *The Looking Glass War*.

Dick Sharples

Dick Sharples has a fine track record as a writer of television comedy, starting with the children's series *Steve Hunter, Trouble Merchant* and including *Joan and Leslie, Hallelujah, The Saint* and *Adam Adamant*. He also devised and wrote the long-running series *General Hospital*.

Dinah Sheridan

Dinah Sheridan has the distinction of being described as the first actress to appear on television when she was seen on *Picture Page* in 1936. Since then she has played numerous television parts, culminating in a seven-year stint in *Don't Wait Up* with Nigel Havers, which ended in 1990. She has worked regularly in the West End and has been a leading lady in British films, where her successes include *Irish and Proud of It*, *Where No Vultures Fly*, *Sound Barrier* and most notably *Genevieve* and *The Railway Children*.

Shaw Taylor

Shaw Taylor began his career as an actor working in live television, before moving on to presenting. He gained nationwide recognition as the regular presenter on *Police Five*, which ran from 1962 until 1990.

Margaret Tabor

Margaret Tabor worked as a stage manager in the theatre before transferring her skills to the realm of live television. She worked for a number of independent companies during the early days of commercial television. She is married to the actor Peter Copley.

Josephine Tewson

Josephine Tewson's best-known role is that of Liz in *Keeping Up Appearances*, although she is also known to many as Mrs H in *Shelley*. Other television work includes *Hark at Barker*, *Wodehouse Playhouse*, *His Lordship Entertains*, *No Appointment Necessary*, *Odd Man Out*, *Tears Before Bedtime* and *Terry and June*. Highlights among her West End credits are *The Real Inspector Hound*, *Habeas Corpus*, *Noises Off* and *Woman in Mind*.

Harry Towb

Harry Towb started acting in Londonderry and has also worked at the Abbey Theatre in Dublin. Amongst his appearances in the West End are *Little Shop of Horrors*, *Anything Goes* and *The Bellow Plays*, which transferred to New York. He has worked for the RSC and the National, most recently in *Death of a Salesman*, *Guys and Dolls* and *Schweyk in the Second World War*. He has been seen on television in *The Camomile Lawn*, *So You Think You've Got Troubles*, *Casualty*, *Brighton Belles* and *The Day Today*. He has written for both BBC Television and Radio.

Margaret Tyzack

Margaret Tyzack has worked in all branches of the theatrical profession – in repertory, the West End, the RSC and in New York. She became widely known on television for her portrayal of Winifred in *The Forsyte Saga* and has also been seen in *The First Churchills*, *Quatermass* and *Cousin Bette*. Her films include *2001*, *The Whisperers*, *A Touch of Love* and *A Clockwork Orange*. In 1970 she was awarded the OBE for services to the theatre.

John Warner

John Warner's early television work included *The Magistrate*, *The Alchemist* and *The Age of Kings*. He appeared in seasons at the Old Vic, the RSC and the National and had the distinction of creating the part of Timothy in the long-running musical *Salad Days*. Among his other television credits were Marlow in *She Stoops to Conquer*, *Mr Bean* and *Terry and June*; he also starred opposite Arthur Lowe in *Potter*. His film career began with *The Cruel Sea* and ended with an appearance in *Without a Clue* starring Michael Caine. He died in 2001.

Colin Welland

Colin Welland's first job in the theatre was in rep, after which he joined the BBC as a newscaster for the northern region. A lead in Granada's *The Verdict Is Yours* led to him being chosen to play PC Graham in *Z Cars*. His other television credits include *Blue Remembered Hills*, *United Kingdom*, *Femme Fatale*, *The Fix*, *Trial and Retribution* and *Bramwell*. His most memorable films are *Yanks*, *Twice in a Lifetime*, *A Dry White Season*, *Dancin' in the Dark* and *Chariots of Fire*, for which he famously won an Oscar – for the screenplay, in his other capacity as a successful writer.

Paul Williamson

Paul Williamson has worked extensively in rep. Among his television credits are *Thorndyke*, *The Jewel in the Crown*, *Keeping up Appearances* and *Hello, Girls*.

Index

Index